3.75

FAMILY

IN

NORTH-WEST
KENT

Clive Cutter

Scarthin Books, Cromford, Derbyshire   1991

FAMILY WALKS
IN NORTH-WEST KENT

Family Walks Series
General Editor: Norman Taylor

––––––––––

THE COUNTRY CODE

Enjoy the countryside and respect its life and work
Guard against all risk of fire
Fasten all gates
Keep your dogs under close control
Keep to public paths across farmland
Use gates and stiles to cross fences, hedges and walls
Leave livestock, crops and machinery alone
Take your litter home
Help to keep all water clean
Protect wildlife, plants and trees
Take special care on country roads
Make no unnecessary noise

––––––––––

Published 1991

Phototypesetting, printing by Higham Press Ltd., Shirland, Derbyshire

ISBN 0 907758 36 3

CHURCH WOOD (Route 3)

Dedication

To Sally.

The Author

Clive Cutter is a keen traveller and writer. Including some work as a freelance journalist, his travels have found him in many occupations from barman and laundryman to teacher and business manager, although his main interest is writing. He lives in Kent with his wife where they enjoy exploring the beautiful countryside.

Acknowledgements

Thanks to Joan Wood and my parents.

CONTENTS

MAP OF THE AREA
Numbers (5 etc.) indicate start of walk

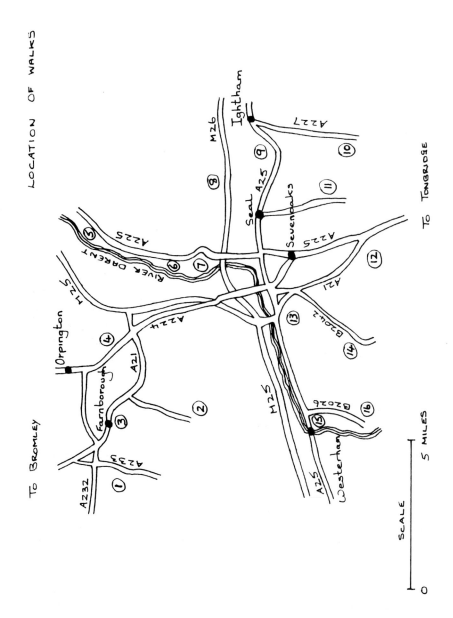

Introduction

North-West Kent.

For the newcomer a venture into the countryside of North-West Kent is likely to result in an exclamation of surprise and delight: "I had no idea there was so much natural beauty so near London!" Having joined the ranks of the initiated they will find it hard to resist further exploration into this lovely corner of the aptly-named Garden of England.

Subsequent visits will unveil a fascinating variety of landscapes -the chalky soil and dominant beech trees along the North Downs Way (which eventually comes out at the white cliffs of Dover), the sweeping Holmesdale Valley, where the River Darent flows leisurely northwards through the charming villages of Otford, Shoreham and Eynsford and then finally, the memorable Greensand Ridge with its buckled meadows and stunning views over the Weald.

The Walks

These walks have been chosen to provide interest and enjoyment for all members of the family. However, it must be said that with the exception of Eynsford, which is suitable even for pushchairs, the hilly terrain means most of the routes are fairly demanding. For most children the prospect of clambering over stiles and crossing little streams via wooden footbridges is all part of the fun. They are also bound to enjoy Oldbury Fort, Ightham Mote and the remains of Eynsford Castle, as well as keeping watch for a wide range of animals and birds. Parents can contemplate the countless generations who have lived in the area from early Stone Age times. The family can share the pleasures of a picnic in an ideal setting or the excitement of visiting the ruins of a Roman villa, one of many beautiful churches or perhaps an historic house such as Knole, Quebec House and Chartwell, which are filled with memorabilia, making entertainment inseparable from education.

Poets and authors have shared a fascination for the county with royalty who, as well as cherishing Kent as a luxurious recreation ground, also appreciated its importance as the first line of defence against any possible attackers from the Continent. The threat today is the same one that faces the whole planet, global warming, and there can be no doubt that the way adults treat their environment will have a direct bearing on their children's future. It is hoped that these walks will help to bring both joy and a greater understanding of the need to protect this beautiful land.

Before you start

Your choice of route will depend on the age and experience of the members of the party and how much time you can allow for the outing. It is wise to allow about an hour per mile for small children, with extra time added on for refreshment and other activities. Try to avoid having to hurry along the final stages of the route. A list of the walks, graded in order of difficulty, is given in the Appendix.

Whatever the weather is like when leaving home it is best to be prepared for rain. Pack some waterproof wear for everyone along with food, binoculars, camera and whatever else you may wish in the rucksacks. A light sweater for everyone is also advisable - you may feel warm when walking and quite chilly when you stop for a picnic. Ideally, every member of the party should carry some share of the burden, so there are no "passengers".

Footwear is important but need not be expensive. On these walks walking boots are not necessary - any strong shoes or trainers will do very well for adults and children. Wellington boots are not recommended though, even if it is likely to be wet underfoot, as they can become very uncomfortable to walk in for any distance.

Most families will probably travel to the start of each walk by car, but information on Public Transport is given at the end of each Route and in the Appendix.

AT KESTON PONDS (Route 1)

6

RAVENSBOURNE NATURE TRAIL

Symbols used on the route maps

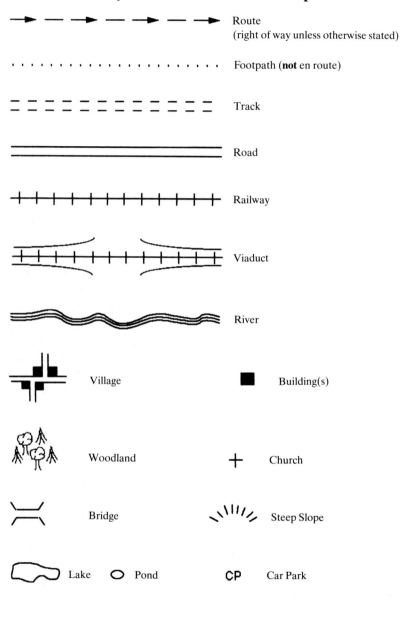

Route
(right of way unless otherwise stated)

Footpath (**not** en route)

Track

Road

Railway

Viaduct

River

Village

Building(s)

Woodland

Church

Bridge

Steep Slope

Lake

Pond

CP Car Park

② etc. corresponds with route description

8

Keston

Outline   Keston Ponds ~ Ravensbourne Nature Trail ~ The Fox ~ Keston Common ~ Keston Ponds.

Summary   This short relaxing walk leads around the beautiful Keston Ponds through the Ravensbourne Nature Trail and past one of the oldest buildings in the area, The Fox, part of several clusters of buildings making up the village of Keston, once known as Chestan. There is so much of interest for all the family that the short distance back to the delightful picnic area on Keston Common could easily take several hours. Children may want to linger to feed the mallards, coots or moorhens, while older members of the family may be happy to sit on one of the many conveniently placed benches and simply enjoy the splendid views. The nature trail is full of picturesque winding paths, wooden steps and little bridges, a constant delight for the youngsters who may also enjoy the almost Disney haunted feel of the gnarled, knobbly oaks in Spring or late Autumn on the exit from the trail near the adventure playground, itself a further source of enjoyment, before the exploration continues.

Attractions   Civilisation has been recorded in Keston as far back as Roman times, although very few roads were made in the area before the 1860's and it was spared the 1930's suburban onslaught that came with the electrification of the railway, a lucky escape probably owing to the prospective costs of cutting through the beautiful hilly terrain. As a result there is a timeless quality about the place, an atmosphere of peace and harmony which is extremely precious, being so close to the concentrated residential streets spreading out from the old market town of Bromley.

History records that an observant soldier saved the Roman camp in nearby Holwood from thirst when he spotted a raven repeatedly swooping to the ground, a subsequent investigation revealing a spring which became known as Caesar's Well. Ravensbourne took its name from the stream, bourn of the raven.

With the charming hospitality available at The Fox and The Greyhound, as well as the occasional ice-cream van in Fishponds Road, it is unlikely that the modern visitor will have to rely on their animal instinct to slake their thirst, although with so much to see, a sharp eye would still be very beneficial. An excellent leaflet on the Ravensbourne Nature Trail is available from libraries and the Bromley Recreation Department which invites children to tick off boxes as they identify plants and trees

continued on page 12

Route 1

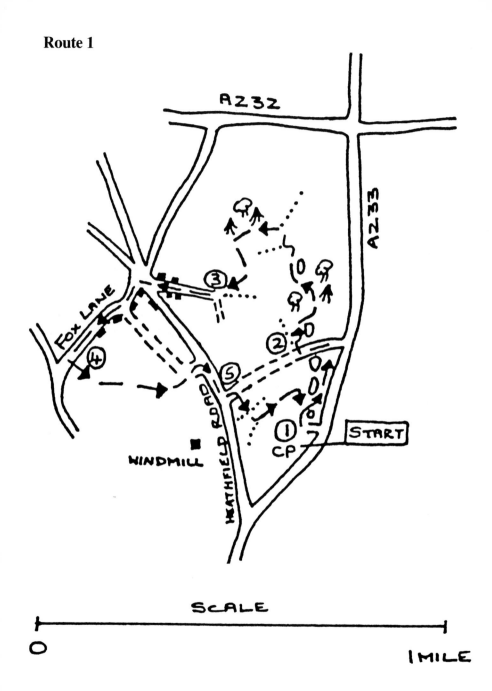

A232

A233

③

Fox Lane

④

②

⑤

HEATHFIELD ROAD

WINDMILL

①
CP

START

SCALE

0

1 MILE

10

Route 1

Keston

2½ miles

START *from Keston Common car park off Westerham Road (A233) (O.S. Pathfinder 1192 G.R. 640420).*

ROUTE

1. *Leave car park via wooden steps down to Caesar's Well and Keston Ponds. Follow path along right bank of two ponds before turning left into Fishponds Road. Continue for about fifty yards before turning right into signposted horsepath. After about ten yards turn right again, descending wooden steps towards pond.*

2. *Having now entered the Ravensbourne Nature Trail, follow numbered red arrow signs along pathway over bridges, beside ponds and along the bank of the stream, turning left after a huge red-barked Wellingtonia (arrow number ten) and crossing a small wooden bridge to go through woodland and into a playing field. Skirt left boundary of field to arrow number thirteen before leaving nature trail by cutting diagonally across the field to the right, reaching a children's adventure playground in the far corner.*

3. *Leave path through wooden gateway and turn right into tarmac footpath leading into Lakes Road. Follow road to intersection with Heathfield Road. Cross over, turn right and then left past the Fox pub into Fox Lane. Follow winding lane down hill before turning left into signposted footpath to Keston Common.*

4. *Continue for a hundred yards before crossing a metal stile. Climb fairly steep path after crossing a second stile to reach Leafy Grove which in turn leads to busy Heathfield Road. Cross over and turn right, continuing across Fishponds Road to enter woodland of Keston Common via a footpath to the left.*

5. *Follow path down slope and up the other side before turning left along pathway into open common. Continue straight across common towards ponds and turn right into pathway leading back to car park.*

ACCESS BY BUS
To Keston from Bromley.

described in sequence with numbered red arrows along the trail. Sadly damage has been caused by the severe gales over recent years, including the felling of a tremendous oak near the wellingtonia, although fortunately nature experts have reported that increased light and dead wood will encourage ground flora, fungi and insects. Many birds can be seen including siskins, wagtails and flycatchers, while a treat on a clear Spring day is the distinctive hammering of woodpeckers echoing through the trees.

On the fairly steep approach back to Leafy Grove and just before re-entering the Common there are several views of the now privately owned post and roundhouse mill, built in 1716 but disused since its sails were damaged in a storm in 1878.

Up until about 50 years ago commoners had grazing rights on Hayes and Keston Commons and since then birch and later oaks have colonised the area. At least one consolation for all the storm damage is that it has performed a natural thinning of the birch trees which, if left uncontrolled, tend to smother the gorse, famous for its beautiful yellow spring blossom and also the heather, a pretty purple in Autumn.

Also on the common are many striking pines and in areas where their canopies allow enough light through to the ground there may be patches of bilberries flowering between April and May and bearing black edible fruits, a plant normally only found in the upland moors of Britain.

Refreshments The Fox and The Greyhound, both with gardens.

DOWN HOUSE

Cudham and Downe

Outline   Cudham ~ Hostye Farm ~ Downe Bank ~ Downe ~ Down House ~ Twenty Acre Shaw ~ Cudham.

Summary   Charles Darwin, author of the Origin of Species and resident of Down House for forty years until his death in 1882, was delighted by the many footpaths in the area, a pleasure modern visitors can still share today. From Cudham, known as Codeham when William the Conqueror gave part of it to the ambitious Odo, Bishop of Bayeux, this fascinating walk includes the beautiful Downe Bank, a Site of Special Scientific Interest. The village of Downe, the central part of which is protected by a conservation order, is full of historical and architectural interest as well as being handy for refreshments at either the Queen's Head, a former grocer's shop, or the George and Dragon, once the post office. Perhaps with heads full of stimulating images from the Darwin Museum in Down House (open afternoons except Mondays and Fridays) children will join parents in a keener observation of the environment on the picturesque return to Cudham which incorporates another Site of Special Scientific Interest called Twenty Acre Shaw.

Attractions   Youngsters will enjoy the wooden steps up and down the escarpment and are likely to have great fun clambering over the numerous stiles along the route, although it must be said that considering the steepness of the slopes and sometimes the height of the stiles, this should be described as a walk for the energetic.

Fortunately the views, particularly along the length of the valley on the descent from Cudham and then again on the return journey, are also numerous and quite refreshing. Early Spring brings the delicate white flowers of the blackthorn and then later various hedgerows, including the striking hawthorn, come alive with blossom. Look out too for the lovely yellow cowslips in Spring, a typical chalk grassland flower.

The seating around the centrally-situated lime tree, which replaced a walnut tree blown down in 1860 and which is now itself a partial victim of storm damage, provides an ideal resting and vantage point in Downe Village with the attractive church on one side and the row of 19th Century houses opposite called Dorset Villas. Other nearby buildings of interest include the Village Hall, built in 1866, Yew Tree Cottages, Walnut Tree Cottage and Walnut Tree House. Trowmers, built in the 18th Century, takes its name from a family who owned land in the area in the 14th Century.

continued on page 16

13

Route 2

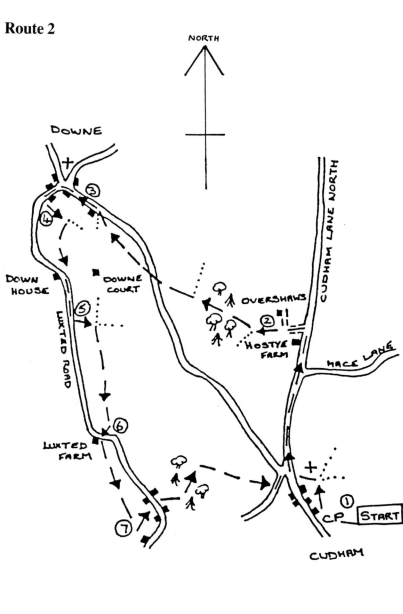

NORTH

DOWNE

③

④

DOWN HOUSE

DOWNE COURT

⑤

LUXTED ROAD

⑥

LUXTED FARM

⑦

OVERSHAWS

CUDHAM LANE NORTH

② II

HOSTYE FARM

MACE LANE

①

CP START

CUDHAM

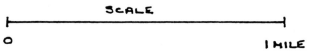

SCALE

0   1 MILE

14

Route 2

Cudham and Downe   4½ miles

START   *at the car park in Cudham Village (O.S. Pathfinder 1208 G.R.*
598445), approached by Cudham Lane North, off the A21.

ROUTE

1. *From the car park follow signposted footpath to the church. Turn left*
   through churchyard and into Church Approach. Turn right and
   continue along Cudham Lane North past Mace Lane, turning left after
   Hostye Farm into driveway with signpost indicating bridleway to
   Downe.

2. *As driveway bears right to Overshaws, continue along bridleway down*
   hill, then climb over a stile to join signposted Cudham Circular footpath
   (CC) to the right. Proceed across valley floor before climbing wooden
   steps up escarpment through woodland. Follow CC shortcut to left
   along a track to Cudham Road. Cross over and turn right, then after
   about ten yards turn left along signposted footpath which borders the
   lane, rejoining it just before Christmas Tree Farm.

3. *Continue past Downe Hall Farm into village as lane becomes High*
   Street Downe. Turn left into Luxted Road, continuing past Forge Croft
   and Snows Cottages before turning left into signposted footpath just past
   Trowmers.

4. *Continue between flint walls and then straight across an open field.*
   Climb over a stile and take a signposted footpath to the right, skirting
   edge of field before passing through a metal kissing gate into another
   field. Cross this field diagonally, before leaving it via another stile and
   turning left into Luxted Road near entrance to Down House.

5. *After several hundred yards, climb a stile on the left into a signposted*
   footpath. Cross a field and then follow footpath sign to the right.
   Continue along track, crossing stile at far right corner of the field. Skirt
   right edge of another field and cross another stile leading into a narrow
   footpath which leads to Luxted Road.

6. *Cross over and turn right. After about ten yards turn left at footpath sign*
   into driveway of Luxted Farm. At end of driveway climb over stile and
   cross a field, keeping to left boundary. Climb a second stile and cross a
   second field, still keeping to the left boundary. Climb a third stile and
   after several hundred yards take a signposted footpath over another stile
   to the left.

7. *Follow narrow footpath to Luxted Road. Cross over, taking footpath*
   opposite through fenced gardens and into woodland. Descend slope via

steep wooden steps and then follow path across open farmland. Climb over another stile and then climb hill. Climb another stile at the top and turn left into Church Hill, continuing up to Cudham Lane. Retrace steps to car park.

ACCESS BY BUS
To Cudham from Orpington.

———

Just outside the village are Down House, Downe Lodge and Downe Court, which is said to be haunted, one of the ghosts being Charles Darwin himself!

The route via the 18th Century Luxted Farmhouse and then alongside the gardens of nearby houses is constantly changing and always appealing, and in Spring or Summer, as the path reaches the top of the wooden steps in Twenty Acre Shaw, the visitor is presented with a glorious tunnel of green foliage dropping away to the valley floor.

Refreshments   At Christmas Tree Farm or the George and Dragon and Queen's Head public houses in Downe and also The Blacksmiths Arms in Cudham.

CLOCKHOUSE FARM

High Elms: Farnborough

Outline Farnborough Village ~ High Elms Estate ~ Wash House Picnic Site ~ Tye Lane ~ Farnborough Village.

Summary Particularly splendid during the sun-drenched days of summer, this is an ever-varied route from the medieval Farnborough Village through the extensive undulating grounds of High Elms Estate. It also makes a wonderful early spring walk for all the family, helping to blow the winter cobwebs away. Sightings of snowdrops, daffodils and crocuses, yellow lesser celandine, as well as the green round buds and lime-coloured hazel catkins make the nature-lover almost taste the rushing change of seasons. Young souls, restless after months of winter restrictions, can climb on fallen trees and explore many little nearby paths in the safe confines of Church Wood and later in the grounds of the estate, where games of chase along the wide wood-chip covered tracks seem irresistible, even for stumbling toddlers.

Attractions The damage caused by the recent terrible storms is heartbreaking to see especially in Church Wood and Mill Hill Wood, although consolation can be taken from the sight of many rows of saplings planted in 1989 by the children of Green Street Green Primary School. This is in keeping with the spirit of John William Lubbock, the 4th baronet and later Lord Avebury, who was inspired by Charles Darwin to collect specimen trees from all over the world. Mature examples of his collection have survived, including two Himalayan and two Atlas cedars, both pairs making an unforgettable greeting at the driveway edge just inside the gates of High Elms Estate. The Atlas cedars take on a remarkable bluish tinge late in Spring.

High Elms Estate, the greater part of which is now a site of scientific interest, became the country house of Sir William Lubbock in 1808 and his descendants lived there until it was sold to the Kent County Council in 1938. The Italian-style mansion built by the 3rd baronet in 1842 was unfortunately burned down in 1967. Still existing is the walled garden, now incorporating a picnic site with a duck pond and chicken run outside a Nature Centre (open at weekends and Wednesday afternoons) with exhibitions including birds' nests, a bird table and information on identifying interesting insects and plants. A sensor course for blind people is being planned. Also still standing is the neighbouring stable yard and the old Eton Fives Court dating from the time of the 4th baronet who was responsible for the introduction of the popular August Bank

continued on page 20

17

Route 3

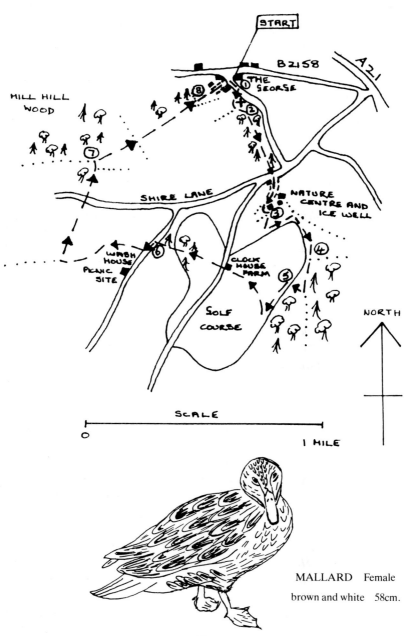

START

B2158

A21

THE GEORGE

HILL HILL WOOD

SHIRE LANE

NATURE CENTRE AND ICE WELL

WASH HOUSE

PICNIC SITE

CLOCK HOUSE FARM

GOLF COURSE

NORTH

SCALE

0   1 MILE

MALLARD   Female
brown and white   58cm.

18

Route 3

High Elms

4½ miles

START *at the George in Farnborough Village (O.S. Pathfinder 1192 G.R. 642444), approached by High Street (B2158), off the A21.*

ROUTE

1. *From the George walk down Church Road for several hundred yards before following a footpath sign along a raised pathway and through a lych gate into the churchyard. Follow path around church and through the graveyard into a field.*

2. *Follow path to the left into Church Wood and continue past the Avebury Memorial and through an avenue of ancient yews to reach Shire Lane. Taking extreme care, cross busy lane to enter High Elms Estate through gateway and walk up drive past Flint Lodge.*

3. *Continue as drive bears left past Eton Fives Court and proceed straight ahead up slope, along a dirt track. On reaching the golf course turn left and continue along path for several hundred yards. At a junction of three pathways turn right and climb slight hill as path leads around the edge of the golfcourse.*

4. *At the top of the hill go straight across another footpath junction, this time going downhill through the woods and down four wooden steps following the path to the right. At a fork in the path turn right again, climbing up to the golfcourse through an old iron gateway.*

5. *Turn left and walk along boundary of golfcourse. On reaching a fenced bridleway turn right and continue along track to reach Clock House Farm. Cross over High Elms Road and follow footpath sign up a hill through another section of golfcourse and more woodland. Continue down the other side of the hill and pass through a wooden gateway before descending further to reach North End Lane.*

6. *Turn left into lane and proceed for several hundred yards before turning right into Bogey Lane. Continue up Bogey Lane for about ten minutes and then follow footpath sign to the right through open farmland to Shire Lane. Cross lane and follow footpath sign along the boundary of a field.*

7. *Leave field at top left corner and follow footpath sign to the right through Mill Hill Wood to open farmland beyond. Continue across field and up hill past thicket and then woodland on the left with open farmland on the right.*

8. *Leave the field as the path bears left before turning sharp right under a metal bar into a tunnelled avenue of pollarded hazels. Continue past*

19

recreation ground and sports fields on the left until path becomes a dirt track called Tye Lane which leads into Church Road opposite The George.

ACCESS BY BUS
To Farnborough from Orpington and Bromley.

———————

Holiday. The Ice Well, probably built in the mid 19th Century and restored as a contribution to the European Agricultural Heritage Year in 1975, was designed to store ice collected from the ponds in winter for domestic use throughout the summer. The well is open to the public on request to the London Borough of Bromley Recreation Department.

In 1826 a wooden tower with a clock and a bell were added to the farm house just off High Elms Road, and it became known as The Clockhouse. Next to it is an early 19th Century octagonal granary built on wooden posts to keep the rats from the grain and now converted into a summer house.

At the corner of North End Lane and Bogey Lane is the site of the old Wash House, once the laundry of the estate and later a rubbish dump until it was saved by the Bromley and District Consumers' Group in 1970 and made into an attractive picnic site.

The final stretch down Tye Lane leads back into Church Road opposite the George of Farnborough, dating from the 16th Century and once used by travellers as a coaching house on their way from London to Hastings.

Refreshments At the George and the Change of Horses in Farnborough.

NEAR CHELSFIELD

Chelsfield Village: Goddington Park

Outline   Goddington Park ~ Lilly's Wood ~ Skeet Hill Lane ~ Chelsfield Village ~ Goddington Park.

Summary   Following an interesting and varied route through gently undulating fields and woodland to the old village of Chelsfield, this is an easy walk for both young and old. During the different seasons of the year there is a constant blaze of colour along the route from the blossoms and wildflowers of spring and the lush green of the summer, to the bright red fruits and the turning leaves of autumn, when hedges and trees are draped in a profusion of wild clematis, known as Old Man's Beard. The rippling fields of wheat in the early summer make an unforgettable sight while other splendid views include the sweeping farmland of Cookham Farm, a majestic row of poplars on the horizon towards Skeet Hill Lane and the valley of Orpington and St. Mary Cray on the approach back into Goddington Park.

Attractions   Goddington House is visible to the left across the park shortly after the beginning of the walk. The estate itself dates back to the Middle Ages when it was owned by the De Godyngton family.

At the Chelsfield Lane entrance to Goddington Park there is a fine example of a cast-iron coal post, painted white and bearing the red shield from the City's arms. Coal posts were erected in the days when boundaries were drawn up to assist with the administration of coal taxes. A second coal post can be seen later in the walk.

Botanists will be enthralled by the carpets of bluebells in the wood during spring, as well as the later buttercups, dandelions and clover in some of the fields. Hedgerows, ablaze with blossom in the early part of the year, are heavy with hips and haws in the autumn. Children will enjoy gathering blackberries in September or juicy clusters of elderberries in the early part of October.

Patience and stealth may be rewarded by occasional sightings of wild rabbits or a fox and along the route there are also plenty of farm animals to be seen such as geese, goats and horses. The whole family can also have fun watching for magpies, finches, bluetits, sparrows and many more.

The embankment near Skeet Hill was created out of rubble from London's bomb damage and was intended to carry the projected orbital road around the capital. This plan was superseded by the M25. The embankment is now home for hawthorn, oak and wild cherry trees.

continued on page 24

Route 4

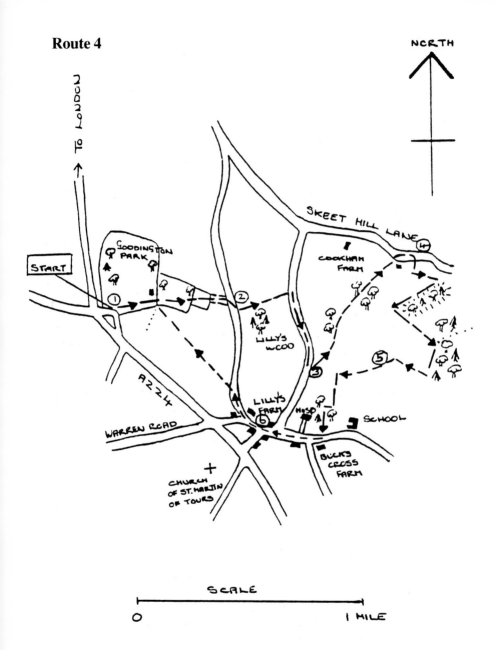

NORTH

TO LONDON

SKEET HILL LANE

START

GOODINGTON PARK

①

④

②

COOKHAM FARM

LILLY'S WOOD

③

⑤

A224

LILLY'S FARM

⑥

WARREN ROAD

WOOD

SCHOOL

BUCKS CROSS FARM

CHURCH OF ST. MARTIN OF TOURS

SCALE

0   1 MILE

Route 4

Chelsfield Village

4½ miles

START   *at the Goddington Park car park (O.S. Pathfinder 1192 G.R. 650472), approached by Court Road (A224).*

ROUTE

1. *From car park walk around playing field towards a pavilion. Follow the lefthand CCW yellow arrow and cross a further two playing fields before leaving the park via a short tarmac avenue of Norway maples.*

2. *Cross over Chelsfield Lane and turn right for several yards. Climb a small wooden staircase on the left to enter a field. Proceed along a path into Lilly's Wood and then into another field. Keep to the lefthand hedgerow to reach a narrow tarmac lane. Turn right and follow lane for about ⅓ mile before reaching a footpath sign on the left.*

3. *Cross over a stile and follow the yellow arrow towards the left across open farmland to a band of woods. Cut through the corner of the woods to a field. Keeping the woods to the left, follow the path to a yellow arrow pointing diagonally across the field to the right. Cross the field and then proceed through another band of woods and across more farmland to reach Skeet Hill Lane.*

4. *Turn right and follow the lane for about 200 yards. Turn right again at a yellow arrow back into the farmland. Follow the yellow arrow around the field and alongside a wooded, man-made embankment. Turn left at the end of the embankment and cross more farmland. On reaching a band of woods follow the yellow arrow to the right for a short distance. Turn right again at a fork in the path marked by yellow arrows.*

5. *Proceed across the edge of several meadows to reach a hedgerow and a narrow farm track. Turn left towards the playing fields of Cannock School. Just before the playing fields turn right at a yellow arrow and walk through a gateway into a tunnelled band of woods. Follow path as it turns left to reach Hawstead Lane. Turn right and follow lane for about a quarter of a mile into Chelsfield Village.*

6. *At the Five Bells Pub turn right into Warren Road. Proceed past Chelsfield Primary School on the right and the Wesleyan Chapel on the left. Turn right into Chelsfield Lane. Follow lane past Lilly's Farm until you reach a footpath sign on the left. Follow direction of yellow arrow across a field and through an ancient hedgerow into Goddington Park. Retrace steps to car park.*

ACCESS BY BUS

To Goddington Park from Orpington.

Throughout the walk pieces of flint can be seen strewn across the fields. There are beautifully preserved flint cottages in Hawstead Lane near Chelsfield Village which is also of tremendous interest. Just beyond a children's playground which backs on to a horse paddock there is a row of 18th and 19th Century cottages, originally the village shops and bakery. The Five Bells Pub, with a beer garden and its own children's playground, makes an ideal resting point before moving on past the schoolhouse of 1864, the neighbouring Cross Hall, possibly from the 16th Century and the Wesleyan Chapel opposite, dated 1872 and now a private residence. Further on is Lilly's Farm, part of which had to be rebuilt after the original 19th Century house was destroyed by a flying bomb in 1944. In addition to the shop, where fresh farm produce can be purchased, there is the Koi Water Barn where colourful Japanese carp are on view and on sale.

Not far from the entrance to the farm in Chelsfield Lane is a huge lime tree - schoolchildren used to race to this tree from their school and the winner, who was then called the King or Queen, had the privilege of sitting in the hollow of the tree.

Refreshments   At the Five Bells Pub in Chelsfield Village.

EYNSFORD

24

Lullingstone: Eynsford

Outline   Eynsford ~ Roman Villa ~ Lullingstone Castle ~ Eynsford Castle ~ Eynsford.

Summary   Nestling comfortably into the Kent countryside is the beautiful old village of Eynsford, in a lush green hollow on the banks of the gently meandering Darent River. A timeless sense of peace and tranquillity is reinforced by the olde-worlde cottages, the almost fable-like turrets of the Lullingstone Gatehouse, the majestic groups of alders, holding court at the river's edge and the elegant sweep of willows on view from the flint ruins of the Norman keep, Eynsford Castle. Delightful scenes merge one into another throughout the length of the valley, with its quietly grazing horses and its watchful yet serene Highland cattle, to the final approach back to the station beneath the cooling leaves of beech, horsechestnut, locust and cherry laurel.

Attractions   The route past the striking buildings of Newbarn Farm and the neat quaintness of the shuttered flint cottage called simply The Cottage, leads over an inviting wooden bridge to the carefully preserved remains of the Lullingstone Roman Villa which provides evidence that this entrancing part of the Darent Valley has been favoured by connoisseurs for centuries.

The beginning of the road to Lullingstone Castle passes alongside the lovely gardens of the Oast House and The Willows which drop away on one side of the road and level out into grazing meadows for horses by the waterside.

Beside the brick and flint stables of the Lullingstone Park Farm, young children can enjoy a close-up view of horses in wooden-fenced paddocks, while older children can also join with the adults in appreciating the vast extent of the landscape, with its undulating lawns and woods, which used to be a deer park but is now a golf course.

The castle, open to the public on Saturdays, Sundays and public holidays (April to October), has been altered considerably since it was first built in the 15th Century. Many of the changes were effected in the 18th Century by the Hart family to please Queen Anne who was a regular visitor. One of the Hart daughters, Anne, named after the queen, is said to have climbed down a rope of knotted sheets to elope with her lover and on his death several years later she returned to Lullingstone to be accepted in marriage by a Sussex gentleman, Sir Thomas Dyke, whom

continued on page 28

25

Route 5

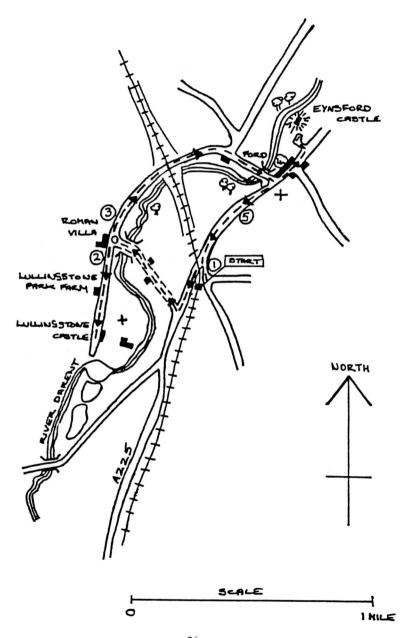

EYNSFORD CASTLE

FORD

ROMAN VILLA ③

④

②

LULLINGSTONE PARK FARM

LULLINGSTONE CASTLE

RIVER DARENT

A225

⑤

① START

NORTH

SCALE

0   1 MILE

26

Route 5

Lullingstone   3½ miles

START   *at Eynsford Station in Station Road (O.S. Pathfinder 1192 G.R. 649537), approached by A225.*

ROUTE

1. *From Eynsford Station turn left. Cross over main road and turn left again. Walk beneath railway bridge and alongside road for several hundred yards. Turn right into private road which is also a footpath indicated by a ground-level concrete sign. Continue along track past Newbarn Farm on the left and The Cottage on the right. Cross over River Darent via a wooden bridge to reach Roman Ruins.*

2. *Turn left at small roundabout. Continue along tarmac lane past Lullingstone Park Farm to the Gatehouse of Lullingstone Castle. Retrace steps to Roman Ruins.*

3. *Continue straight along lane, passing beneath viaduct. Bearing right, continue past Home Farm and Toll Bar Cottage to reach the Ford.*

4. *Cross over Ford bridge and turn left into main road. Proceed through village, turning left at sign for Eynsford Castle. Retrace steps from castle.*

5. *Continue straight along main road past church to reach railway station.*

ACCESS BY BUS AND TRAIN
To Eynsford from Dartford by bus and from Bromley South by train.

BEECH NUTS

she had previously jilted. Descendants of the Hart Dyke family still live in the castle today.

From the idyllic hedgerowed track between the Roman villa and the enormous arches of the viaduct, a lucky visitor may spot a speeding kingfisher or perhaps a heron standing motionless beneath the bank alders at the water's edge. Just past the viaduct, children will love the woolly Highland cattle kept as pets in the riverside grounds of Home Farm, which is bordered by the lawns and the conifer plantation of the Water Board.

Further on is the extremely crooked Toll Bar Cottage where a charge used to be made to users of Sparepenny Lane, a shortcut from Farningham. The green bank and the public house at the Ford are a popular haunt in the summer and the Ford House Tea Shop just across the bridge is a must for those with a fond weakness for home-made cream teas.

Refreshments   Ford House Tea Shop, Lullingstone Gatehouse Teashop and a variety of pubs and restaurants.

THE DARENT AT SHOREHAM

Shoreham

Outline   Shoreham Station ~ Shoreham Village ~ The Terrace ~
Filston Stream ~ Shoreham Station.

Summary   Shoreham was described as a "valley of vision" by the great
artist Samuel Palmer during the early part of the 19th Century. He and his
friends, including the ever-inspiring William Blake, delighted in the
simple rustic scenes of life in the area. Calling themselves the Ancients,
they scorned modern materialism, preferring instead the values of Merry
Old England. Since then the caring attentions of many local groups,
including the Women's Institute and the Shoreham Society, have ensured
that urban influences have been kept at bay.

    This walk around and through the village has many stiles to climb
and two steep hillside ascents, making it a fairly demanding route.
However, the effort is compensated by a variety of splendid views.

Attractions   While adults will immediately be impressed by the view of
the valley from Station Road, including the tower of the church peeping
above the tree-tops and the huge white cross dug into the chalk of the
western hillside by local residents in memory of those killed in the First
World War, the children in the group will regard this particular walk as an
exciting adventure playground. The challenging height of the stiles, the
long narrow pathways and the fairytale stretches of banks beside the
streams and rivers will keep them enthralled. Farm animals can be seen as
well as wilder animals more likely in the older woodland above The
Terrace, like rabbits, voles, squirrels, foxes, badgers and perhaps even
fallow deer. Birdwatchers have recorded sightings of three species of
woodpecker, as well as jays and goldcrests in these woods. The young
adventurer will be pleased to hear that one of only four shops in the
village is a most inviting sweet and toy shop. Just above the High Street,
in a recreation ground flanked by magnificent beeches and forming a
picnic spot with views beyond comparison, there are also two children's
playgrounds, the second offering a climbing frame and swings for the very
young.

    The Church of St. Peter and St. Paul was built in 1755 although some
parts date back to the 13th Century. Entry to the churchyard, from either
a swing gate at the back (on the route of the walk) or through the front
lych gate of 1862, presents the visitor with a beautiful pathway made of
100-year-old paving stones, re-laid in 1982 by locals and bordered on both

continued on page 32

Route 6

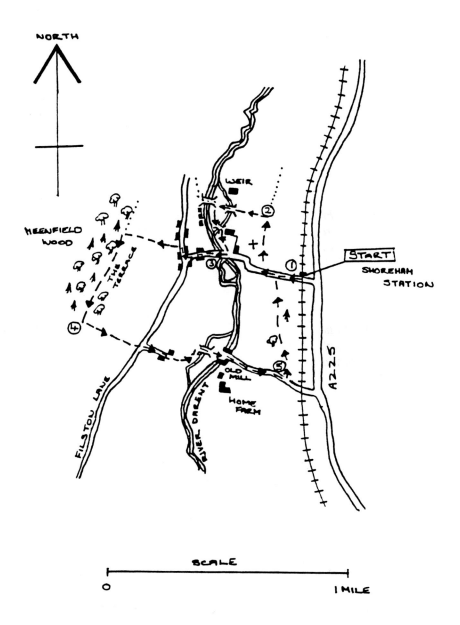

NORTH

MEENFIELD WOOD

THE TERRACE

WEIR

START
SHOREHAM STATION

A225

FILSTON LANE

RIVER DARENT

OLD MILL

HOME FARM

① ② ③ ④ ⑤

SCALE

0   1 MILE

Route 6

Shoreham 4 miles

4 miles

START *from Shoreham Station (O.S. Pathfinder 1192 G.R. 615526) off the A225.*

ROUTE

1. *Walk down steps to the left of the station car park. Turn right into lane (Station Road) and proceed for several hundred yards. At stone footpath sign turn right into field. Follow track to stile on the left just past churchyard. Cross over stile and continue along narrow path to another stile leading into a field. Walk straight along edge of field before climbing over a third stile.*

2. *Turn left and follow path, crossing over wooden stile. Continue along path and over Filston Stream via small footbridge. Bear right to end of path and then cross stile on the left. Turn left again just before the bridge at yellow arrow indicating Darent Valley Path. Walk along path beside river to reach War Memorial on right. Turn right over bridge into Church Street.*

3. *Continue through village to T-junction. Turn right into High Street and proceed for fifty yards. Turn left at footpath signs for Halstead and Timberden Bottom. Climb hill past recreation ground, through narrow hedgerowed path, over stile and across a field to reach a stile at the fringe of Meenfield Woods. Cross stile, turn left and follow footpath known as The Terrace along the side of the hill and through a small section of woods to reach another stile.*

4. *Cross stile and turn left into field. Descend hill to reach another wooden stile. Cross over stile and walk down track, continuing over tarmac road into a public bridlepath, which in turn leads into a narrow footpath. Proceed along the bank of Filston Stream and over footbridge into a lane. Follow lane uphill past The Old Mill (the River Darent is visible in the grounds on the right before disappearing into a culvert). Continue straight on past Home Farm and then through the golfcourse.*

5. *Turn left at wooden sign with yellow arrow pointing towards Shoreham. Follow path through golfcourse to reach Station Road. Turn right and retrace steps to station.*

ACCESS BY BUS AND TRAIN
To Shoreham from Sevenoaks by bus and from Bromley South by train.

sides by rows of Irish yews planted in 1867, particularly striking with their red berries in the autumn. Inside the church there is a painting depicting the return of Lieutenant Cameron of the Royal Navy who crossed Africa from west to east in search of Doctor Livingstone. The pulpit, brought from Westminster Abbey in 1851, was used at Queen Victoria's coronation and the organ, also from the Abbey, was used at the coronation of George II.

Both the riverside garden of Samuel Palmer's old home, the Water House, and the sycamore-shrouded white weather-boarding of the Samuel Palmer School of Fine Art can be seen along the walk, as well as the 16th Century public house called the King's Arms, which boasts the only remaining ostler's box in the country. Messages and tankards of ale were passed through a window to the ostler who looked after the customer's horses.

In the ancient Meenfield Woods a rich shrub layer includes hazel, hawthorn, guelder rose, dogwood, travellers' joy and honeysuckle. The tall pink flowers of the rosebay willow herb and the lilac creeping thistle are also in evidence, while on the valley floor, along the bank of the Filston Stream, enthusiasts can enjoy identifying the medieval salad plant, watercress, together with the pink lantern-type flowers of Indian balsam.

Refreshments   Various pubs and the Shoreham Countryside Society for home-made cakes and teas.

VILLAGE POND, OTFORD

32

Otford

Outline Otford Village ~ River Darent ~ Greenhill Wood ~ Otford Mount ~ Otford Village.

Summary When King Henry VIII received Otford Palace, an obligatory gift from Archbishop Cranmer in 1537, he spurned it as being too damp. While it would do for the other members of his household, he himself would on future visits stay at Knole in Sevenoaks. This interesting account can hardly be taken as the final word on the village which wears a rich mantle of historical interest and natural beauty with a regal authority all of its own. History also records that Thomas a Becket once lashed out impatiently with his staff and a healing spring gushed from the ground. For the architectural enthusiast strolling down the High Street, or the artist inspired by the many far-reaching views; for the botanist comparing the flora between the downlands and the differing ridge of clay with flints on the crest of the downs; or for the youngsters sharing the joy of generations of children playing amongst the tangled roots and the steep slopes of the old chalk pit, Otford still offers a feeling of magic, usually reserved only for legend.

Attractions Otford, known as Stumbleburrow in medieval times, was taken from the Saxons by Otta, King of Mercia, and given to the church in the 11th Century, making it one of twenty-five manors owned by the Archbishop of Canterbury. Evidence of earlier human habitation dates back about two thousand years and it is now designated as a Special Landscape Area with sites of Special Scientific Interest.

To the left on leaving the car park is Church Hall, built in 1910 by Sir Edwin Lutyens and opposite is The Bull, with Tudor fireplaces and a wishing chair which reputedly belonged to Thomas a Becket. Just past the school is the Old Parsonage, one of the oldest dwellings in Otford. The Mill House and the Little Oast, a converted Victorian hop kiln, form a beautiful introduction to the walk along the restful River Darent with sweeping views of Polhill to the left, Greenhill to the right and in the distance the memorial chalk cross on the hillside of Shoreham.

The ascent of Greenhill is very steep, although the views from the top and along the ridge to Otford Mount are spectacular, the green grass of the valley dotted in early spring with bright yellow outcrops of forsythia. The walk across the ridge, first on a track and then along a quiet lane, leads past several farms including Paine's Farm, dating from the Middle Ages and its contrasting modern neighbour, Mount Farm. Both

continued on page 36

Route 7

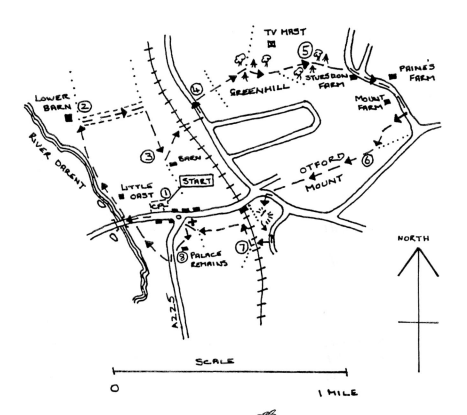

TV MAST

GREENHILL

STURSDON FARM

⑤

PAINE'S FARM

MOUNT FARM

LOWER BARN ②

RIVER DARENT

③

BARN

START

LITTLE OAST ①

OAST

OTFORD MOUNT

⑥

④

⑦

⑧ PALACE REMAINS

A225

NORTH

SCALE

0

1 MILE

FOXGLOVE
purple, white or yellow
June-Sept.

34

Route 7

Otford   5 miles

START *from car park in Otford High Street (O.S. Pathfinder 1208 G.R. 593525) off A225.*

ROUTE

1. *Turn right from car park into High Street. Continue for about five hundred yards past The Horns public house. Turn right at yellow arrow and follow Darent Valley Path beside Little Oast and then along river bank to Lower Barn.*

2. *At Lower Barn turn right and walk along track between open farmland before turning right again at a T-junction and proceeding for several hundred yards along another track.*

3. *Turn left into footpath just before a large barn and continue diagonally across field and then over stile to cross railway line. Cross a second stile to enter narrow hedgerowed path which leads to Shoreham Road. Taking care of traffic, cross road and turn left, continuing for two hundred yards.*

4. *Turn right, crossing over stile into footpath indicated by yellow arrow. Climb long steep slope between farm fields and meadows to reach woodland at the top of Greenhill. Follow path into woods, taking right-hand fork after about twenty yards and continue through a small band of woods to reach grassland. Follow path upwards and to the left along the edge of the woods to reach a small plateau beside the television mast.*

5. *Take track at top right corner through woodland past Stursdon Farm, turning right into tarmac lane. Continue past Paine's Farm on left and Mount Farm on right before taking a right-hand footpath leading through a band of woods and across the corner of a field into the North Downs Way.*

6. *Descend North Downs Way via a series of wooden steps to reach Pilgrim's Way. Cross over and turn right. After about ten yards turn left into Chalk Pit and follow path which skirts a playing field and turns right to reach a tarmac path. Turn left and follow path to the end, turning right along street for about twenty yards before turning right again into another tarmac footpath. Climb stile to cross railway line.*

7. *Climb another stile and turn right, follow path to a T-junction and turn left away from the station. Follow path through churchyard to War Memorial and village pond. Turn sharp left towards Otford Palace remains and then turn right into Palace Field along tarmac pathway.*

8. *At end of pathway cross over A225 and turn left for several yards before following a footpath to the right which leads into Pickmoss Lane and then the High Street. Retrace steps to car park.*

ACCESS BY BUS AND TRAIN

To Otford from Sevenoaks by bus and from Bromley South by train.

---

young and older members of the family can enjoy keeping watch for a wide range of animals.

Also in spring, listen for the distinctive chirrup of the greenfinch, although a glimpse requires stealth and silence. Bluetits, robins and wrens can also be seen along with many flowers including daffodils, snowdrops, crocuses, primroses, sweet violets, lesser celandine, wood anemone and grape hyacinths. The delicate fluffy catkins of the sallow or pussy willow are an unforgettable sight. So too are the new leaves of the weeping willows beside the spring-filled village pond, lit up with a golden glow on a welcome sunny day.

Refreshments   At The Bull or The Crown public houses - both cater for children.

NEARLY CORNER, HEAVERHAM

Route 8

Kemsing

Outline   Kemsing ~ St. Edith's Farm ~ Heaverham ~ North Downs Way ~ Kemsing.

Summary   Travellers taking the ancient Pilgrims' Way to Canterbury used to stop in Kemsing on the southern slopes of the North Downs to pay tribute to St. Edith, a lady born in the village in 996 and known for her exceptional piety. Local farmers brought their grain to be blessed at a shrine in her name in the churchyard, hoping for a bountiful harvest. For more contemporary travellers the M26 on the other side of the village makes it possible to speed straight past, a blessing for pressurised businessmen, although a wasted opportunity for those with the time to enjoy the bountiful views and the quaint atmosphere of peace and harmony which is reinforced by several age-old buildings and lends weight to the spiritual significance of the area. Of course reports of ghosts stalking the family-orientated Wheatsheaf are nonsense. Aren't they? Parents may ponder over a glass of ale or maybe even a firsthand account, while children let their imaginations run riot in other directions as they enjoy playing in the creatively-designed pub garden.

Attractions   Near the car park of this former Saxon settlement is the huge St. Edith's Hall, built in 1911, with a thought-provoking message on its clock-tower: Tis mine each passing hour to tell, tis thine to use it ill or well. As visitors proceed on this walk of contrasts beneath a second clock hung from the weatherboard wall of Little Wybournes and then past the neat timber-framed St. Edith's Farm Cottage, they are confronted by inviting open farmland. The coniferous woodland across the field is deliciously fragrant and there is a splendid view of Otford Mount away towards the right.

For some the noisy traffic on the M26, flanking the footpath for about half a mile, may become slightly oppressive. However, as the route begins its gentle descent into the quiet hamlet of Heaverham, any discomfort is soon forgotten. From beneath a spreading chestnut tree halfway down the hill it is possible to see the 15th Century hall house of Broughton over to the right, while towards the left is the yellow brickwork of the double-storey 19th Century Crowdleham. Directly ahead is the garden of the Manor House and to the left of that the tops of two oasts which form part of a 19th Century building adjacent to Nearly Corner. On the hillside beyond is the enormous country house of St. Clere.

continued on page 40

Route 8

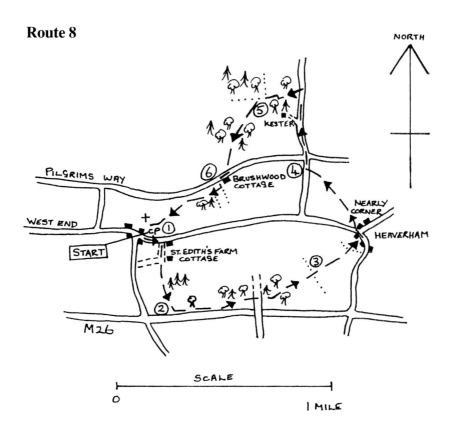

NORTH

PILGRIMS WAY

WEST END

START

CP ①

St. Edith's Farm Cottage

M26

② ③ ④ ⑤ ⑥

BRUSHWOOD COTTAGE

KESTER

NEARLY CORNER

HEAVERHAM

SCALE

0   1 MILE

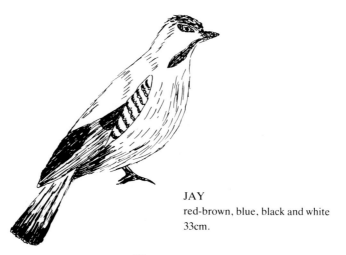

JAY
red-brown, blue, black and white
33cm.

Route 8

Kemsing

4½ miles

START *at the Kemsing Village Car Park in the High Street (O.S. Pathfinder 1208 G.R. 587556), approached by Pilgrim's Way off the A225.*

ROUTE

1. *Turn left from car park into High Street. Continue past St. Edith's Hall and The Old Forge before turning right into a track beside Little Wybournes. Continue past Ark View and at driveway to St. Edith's Farm Cottage, where track bears right, cross fence using stone steps and continue across open field towards wood. Cross over stile into another field and continue beside coniferous woodland on the left for about a hundred yards. Proceed straight across open field to far left corner beside the motorway.*

2. *Cross two stiles in quick succession into field and keeping to right edge continue parallel to motorway. Just before bridge climb stile on left into woodland and follow path, crossing another stile, a road and then a third stile into a further band of woodland. Proceed straight across an open field and cross another stile. Follow direction of footpath sign diagonally across farmland, continuing between two wooden posts and beneath a horse chestnut tree across a further section of farmland.*

3. *At intersection of four footpaths take path straight ahead between a hedgerow and a garden. At end of footpath go through white gate shared with Walnut Tree Cottage, leading into lane. Turn left and continue past Nearly Corner before taking a footpath to the right leading diagonally across open farmland.*

4. *Leave farmland on far side between gap in hedgerow and turn right into lane. Continue straight over crossroads and climb lane in direction fo East Hill and Eynsford. After about half a mile, at the second gateway to Kester, turn left over stile into North Downs Way. After several hundred yards cross two closely-situated stiles indicated on the right and then turn left, skirting the edge of a field and leaving it by climbing another stile in the far left corner.*

5. *After twenty yards turn left over stile and cross open field diagonally towards the right, before crossing another stile into a footpath leading downhill through trees. Climb another stile and proceed diagonally across right corner of a field, before entering woodland over a further stile. Continue along footpath before crossing a stile and turning right into a lane.*

6. *Continue for fifty yards and then turn left into a bridleway beside Brushwood Cottage. After only a few yards turn right up a small stairway and proceed straight along track between trees to reach common. Cross common to children's playground and church on far side. Leave common via wooden gate and enter churchyard. Follow path through churchyard and exit via a lych gate leading to car park.*

ACCESS BY BUS
To Kemsing from Sevenoaks.

———

On entering the hamlet, closer inspection reveals the charm of the 16th Century Walnut Tree Cottage, built with Kentish ragstone at the front and with flint at the back. A pleasant diversion may be made at this point to the Georgian Chequers pub.

To climb to join the North Downs Way is steep, although there is plenty of cooling shade from the beautiful yew trees along the way. The views over the farmland in the valley on the subsequent descent of the North Downs are magnificent and if the temptation for a picnic on an open area halfway down the slope can be resisted, then the wide and picturesque Kemsing Common at the bottom will prove ideal. Should children have any energy left after climbing all the many stiles or romping in and out of woods, and if they are unimpressed by the playground near the church, there is a simple solution: tell them quite literally to go fly a kite! The setting is perfect!

Refreshments At the Bell or Wheatsheaf in Kemsing and at the Chequers in Heaverham.

STYANTS WOOD

40

Route 9

Oldbury Hill

Outline   Styants Wood ~ Oldbury Hill ~ Fish Ponds Wood ~ Styants Wood.

Summary   Children will love the steep winding steps up the slopes of this Iron Age fort, although some of the older members of the family might jokingly suggest going back instead and making an early start on the perfect picnic which may be planned for their return at one of the tables in a quiet corner near the car park. However, any reluctance or twinges of fatigue should soon be forgotten as they stroll leisurely beneath the trees high up on the side of Oldbury Hill. Around the corner is a mediaeval road flanked by a picturesque private farm and then a sloping prehistoric track through open spaces of fern and dotted woodland, predominantly oak. After exploring the beautiful Fish Ponds Wood, (taking care of the steep drop to the left of the path along the ridge), a glass of real ale at the Crown Point Inn may prove very tempting. There is also an imaginative children's playground in the well-appointed pub garden.

Attractions   The first known visitors to Oldbury Hill are thought to have been early Stone Age people who probably only used the area for hunting rather than habitation. Later Stone Age people are thought to have used rocks and caves for rudimentary shelter. Next came the Wealden people, eventually reaching Oldbury around the 1st Century B.C. via a prehistoric track through the Weald, after crossing the Channel from France and landing in Sussex about two centuries earlier. The threat of attack from the Belgae tribe in about 20 A.D. made them fortify their settlement with a ditch and wooden stockade and although these measures proved inadequate when the onslaught actually came, it is believed that the two tribes managed to live on peaceably together. At least until the Romans arrived in about 40 A.D., when they overran the renewed fortifications to take possession of the fort, even though they never appeared to live there themselves.

Today's inhabitants of Oldbury Hill, protected by their champion, The National Trust, include wood mice, bank voles and the highly organised and always busy wood ants, the largest type to be found in Britain. Although perhaps not everyone's dream-come-true, the sight of an ants nest, a seething mound of industry, is quite intriguing. Don't worry - the National Trust assures us that the ants do not have a particularly nasty bite!

continued on page 44

Route 9

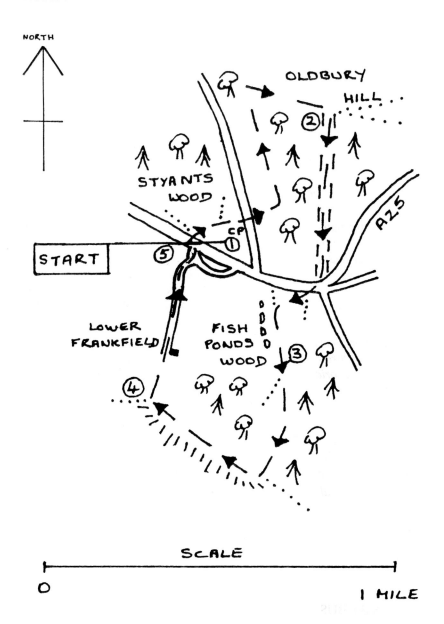

NORTH

OLDBURY
HILL

STYANTS
WOOD

A25

CP

START ⑤ ①

②

LOWER
FRANKFIELD

FISH
PONDS
WOOD ③

④

SCALE

0   1 MILE

42

Route 9
Oldbury Hill

4 miles

START   *at car park and picnic site in Styants Wood off Styants Bottom Road (O.S. Pathfinder 1208 G.R. 558579), approached by the A25 opposite the Crown Point Inn.*

ROUTE

1. *Leave the car park and picnic area via the exit and cross over Styants Bottom Lane, climbing a steep slope along a footpath directly opposite. Continue up wooden steps, turning left at a junction near the top of the hill. Proceed along wide path, eventually bearing right just before a steep gully. Follow this Mediaeval Highway to a junction of three paths.*
2. *Take right path and continue along grassy prehistoric trackway as it slopes gently up the hill. Keep straight ahead until path crosses the brow of the hill and descends the other side, reaching the busy A25. Cross over carefully and turn right. After fifteen yards turn left into a footpath leading through Fish Ponds Wood. Turn right at fork in path and then left on reaching a T-junction. Proceed past a series of ponds on the right, continuing into woods as path becomes a sandy bridleway.*
3. *Keep to bridleway as it swings uphill to the left and continue climbing a steep slope through woods, eventually reaching a T-junction. Turn right into another bridleway and continue along ridge with steep drop to the left (children must be very careful along this stretch).*
4. *On reaching a wooden gate to the right of the path, turn right, passing beside the gate and proceeding downhill in the direction of a stone sign indicating a public bridleway. Follow path which comes out behind Lower Frankfield and leads into a lane. Continue along length of lane between fields, turning left at a T-junction into another lane.*
5. *Continue for about twenty yards to busy T-junction with Sevenoaks Road (A25) and cross over, following footpath opposite down the hill into Styants Wood. Continue through woods and on reaching an intersection, turn right along path leading through picnic area back to car park.*

ACCESS BY BUS
To Crown Point Inn from Sevenoaks.

Throughout the route, shrouded in many places with oak, beech, Scots pine, rowan and holly, the sound of birdsong is always present. The area is a haven for blackcaps, chaffinches, starlings, woodpeckers and nuthatches. In season there are delightful outcrops of dog rose, yellow buttercups in the grass and tall purple foxgloves amongst the ferns. Across the A25, beside the extremely peaceful and lovely ponds, a startled grass snake may slither from a quiet sun trap on the bank, disappearing quickly into the reeds. Butterflies may flit unexpectedly across the path.

At six hundred feet above sea level, the south gate is the highest point of the fort, which has an overall area of about a hundred and twenty acres and a circumference of two and a half miles. Lovely views suddenly open out through the trees at various other high points along the walk, especially from the ridge at the bottom of Fish Ponds Wood, which offers breath-taking glances over a canopy of tree tops in the valley below.

Refreshments   At the Crown Point Inn or a picnic in the site near the car park.

FATTING PEN

44

Shipbourne

Outline Shipbourne ~ Fatting Pen ~ Ightham Mote ~ Fairlawne ~ Shipbourne.

Summary History, outstanding natural beauty and a curious tale of the supernatural combine to make this a fascinating and pleasurable walk through an idyllic part of the Kent landscape. From the sparsely dotted buildings of Shipbourne, pronounced Shibbun, deriving its name from the practice of washing sheep in the stream, the route draws its visitors almost hypnotically northwards past the Victorian St. Giles church, with its beautiful Italian mosaic floor, through the amusingly-named woodlands of Fatting Pen, to reach the manor house of Ightham Mote, which means the meeting place. It then returns southwards through the splendid grounds of the famous 17th Century Fairlawne, the garden streams and ponds below it fed by the same spring waters that run beside the 14th Century walls of the moat. Children can enjoy trying to match the regular cries of pheasants with an actual colourful sighting of the bird or perhaps look out for squirrels in the woods and sheep grazing in the fields, possibly with their little lambs at their sides. Many wide and safe pathways and tracks are ideal for running and exploring.

Attractions Local feelings ran high in 1662 at the unfair execution on Tower Hill of Sir Harry Vane, former owner of Fairlawne, who had apparently exasperated Oliver Cromwell to the point where the Lord Protector, as he was known, begged the Lord for deliverance from the man. The detailed arrangements were in fact taken care of by mere mortals and were not left to the judgement of the Almighty and it is said that the restless ghost of Harry Vane, head held under his arm, walks in the gardens of Fairlawne to this very day. Among those who visit his coffin in the crypt of the local church are many Americans, a result of his popular position as Governor of Massachusetts for two years during the earlier part of his life.

Another famous resident of Shipbourne and the subject of yet another tragic story was the poet Christopher Smart, born in 1722, who wrote his only acclaimed work, The Song of David, in charcoal on the wall of a mental institution, a destination reached by all accounts through dedicated drunkenness.

Also a former owner of Fairlawne was Edward Cazalet, who in 1880 gave the village its church and the Chaser pub which overlooks the common. One of his descendants started the famous racing stable and

continued on page 48

Route 10

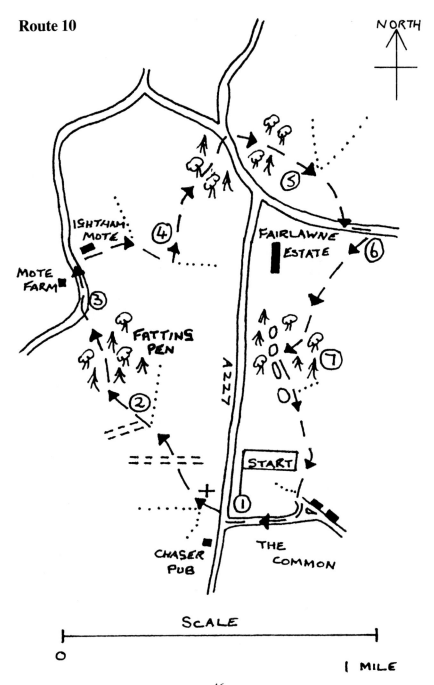

NORTH

ISHTHAM MOTE

MOTE FARM

③

FATTINS PEN

②

A227

④

FAIRLAWNE ESTATE

⑤

⑥

⑦

START

①

CHASER PUB

THE COMMON

SCALE

0   1 MILE

46

Route 10

Shipbourne

4½ miles

START   *at Upper Green Road beside the common in Shipbourne (O.S. Pathfinder 1208 G.R. 522592), off the A227. Park on verge.*

ROUTE

1. *From the common walk along Upper Green Road towards St. Giles church. Cross A227 and walk through the churchyard, leaving it through a gate before turning right into a footpath. Continue along the edge of a field, leaving it at the far right-hand corner, which is marked by a yellow painted wooden post. Continue straight along a footpath across another field, again leaving it at the far right-hand corner, also marked by a yellow post.*

2. *Turn left along a track through another field, passing a further yellow post, as the path bears right, and then cross a stile into Fatting Pen woodland. Proceed through woods, crossing over a track on the way before crossing a stile into another field. Skirt the right-hand edge of this field, leaving it by crossing a further stile into yet another field. Continue along the left edge of this field to reach a lane.*

3. *Turn right into lane for several hundred yards, passing Mote Farm on the left before entering Ightham Mote through an iron gateway. Follow the driveway as it bends to the right past the house and then climbs a hill. Continue straight ahead as the driveway becomes a track, leading through several fields. After about half a mile turn left into a footpath which is clearly visible through a wooden gate.*

4. *Follow footpath along the edge of several fields, finally entering woodland through a gateway. Continue through woodland, eventually leaving it through another gateway before turning right into a lane. After about ten yards turn left into a public bridleway which leads through another gateway into Fairlawne Estate. Continue through woods, leaving them through another gate which leads into an open field.*

5. *Continue along the right-hand boundary of the field, turning right at a fork in the footpath before crossing over a stile into another field. Skirt the left boundary of the field, leaving it at the far left corner by crossing over a stile into a lane. Turn left and after several hundred yards climb a stile on the right back into the grounds of Fairlawne.*

6. *Bear slightly to the right and proceed via two further stiles, continuing downhill in the direction of another yellow post, which leads to yet another stile marked again by a yellow post. A further yellow post and a*

further marked stile lead out of Fairlawne and down a short slope to a tarmac track beside a row of ponds.

7. *Turn left in the direction indicated by a footpath sign to Shipbourne. Keep to the right at a fork in the track, passing the old mill house on the right before going through a wooden gateway. Follow path and cross a stream via a small concrete bridge. Continue uphill through a field towards houses. Keep straight on as footpath forks to the right and proceed between gardens to reach a tarmac driveway. Bearing right, follow driveway and lane back to the common.*

ACCESS BY BUS
To Shipbourne from Tonbridge.

————

later Major Peter Cazalet trained horses for the Queen Mother. In 1932 the major married the daughter of P. G. Wodehouse and it is thought that the author's Shipley Hall, fictional home of Lord Uffingham, was based on Fairlawne.

There is today no fiction in the claim that the grounds are magnificent and the writer Arthur Mee will not be alone with his fond preference for the time of year when the gorgeous rhododendrons are in blossom.

Throughout the walk there is a generous offering of panoramic view over rolling hills and dales with numerous oaks and occasional clumps of chestnut and elegant Scot's pine. Together with the oak and pine woodland of Fatting Pen and the huge beeches at the walk's entrance to Fairlawne, these provide plenty of cooling shade at regular intervals.

Also lovely to see are the pretty examples of the Kent oasthouse, several providing private homes in heavenly settings. There is much fun to be had too from trying to identify the many wildflowers, butterflies and birds along the way, while the wonderfully English sight of Ightham Mote in the peaceful depths of the countryside may well inspire family members of all ages.

Refreshments At the Chaser or a picnic in one of many ideal spots on the route.

One Tree Hill

Outline   One Tree Hill ~ Carter's Hill ~ Knole Park ~ Fawke Common ~ Bitchet Common ~ One Tree Hill.

Summary   This fairly short and largely undemanding walk starts at the spectacular vantage point of One Tree Hill on the Greensand Ridge, which offers far-reaching views across the Vale of Kent to the High Weald beyond. An occasional wild pheasant may be spotted taking a stroll of its own on Carter's Hill, while on certain days a more organised animal display in the form of a gymkhana may be enjoyed on a field belonging to Absaloms Farm. Children are bound to be delighted at a lucky sighting of little fawns peeping from their hiding places in the bracken of Knole Park and a visit to the historic house itself, with its displays of art, furniture and silver, should leave adults enthralled. In Spring wildflowers abound, possibly more so because of the loss of many trees in recent storms.

Attractions   The summit of One Tree Hill is believed to have been the site of a Roman cemetery, although there are no visible remains today. The name is apparently derived from an original beech tree and in spite of serious storm damage there are in fact many trees in the area. Particularly notable is the fascinating variety, including rowan, holly, birch, yew and of course the stately beech, which can all be found in Fawke Common, deriving its name from the Richard la Ffalke family in the 14th Century.

Bluebells and primroses will make a lasting impression on flower-lovers as they saunter through the woodland of Carter's Hill, named after Richard Carter, Constable of Codsheath Hundred in 1450. A sharp eye might catch a glimpse of a tree creeper before it scurries around the trunk of a tree like a squirrel, safely out of sight. An attempt at some stealthy woodcreeping by the observer might reveal the long-beaked bird clinging silently to the bark on the other side. Other birds to look out for are robins, woodpeckers, nuthatches and also the beautiful redstarts which usually return to breed in the south east part of Knole Park at the end of April.

The entry on this walk into Knole Park provides instant evidence of the destructive force of the terrible storms that have hit Britain in recent years. Huge beech trees were wrenched out by the roots and flung to the ground as if by some bad-tempered giant. Fortunately the line of chestnuts that lend their name to Chestnut Walk are some of the few survivors. New hope also lies in the many young saplings planted in the

continued on page 52

49

Route 11

NORTH

FAWKE FARM HOUSE

KNOLE PARK

④

⑤

③

①

CP

START

②

CARTER'S HILL HOUSE

SCALE

0   1 MILE

ELDERBERRY

50

Route 11

One Tree Hill   3 miles

START   *at the One Tree Hill car park off Park Lane (O.S. Pathfinder 1208 G.R. 532559), approached by A25.*

ROUTE

1. *Follow a signposted footpath leading from the right-hand corner of the car park. At a T-junction just over the brow of the hill turn right and continue to a stile which leads into a lane. Turn left into lane and proceed for about fifty yards, passing Carter's Hill House on the left before turning right into the driveway of Shepherd's Mead. After about ten yards turn right into a signposted footpath.*

2. *At the end of this path climb over a stile and turn right into a bridleway. After only several yards turn left to cross another stile into a field. Skirt the left edge of this field and at the far side turn right, again skirting the edge of the field before crossing another stile on the left to enter woodland. Continue through woodland, eventually crossing a stile into a lane.*

3. *Cross lane and pass through a gateway directly opposite into Knole Park. After about fifty yards turn right into a tarmac track and continue to end. Proceed straight ahead along a dirt track which narrows to a path after about twenty yards.*

4. *On reaching a fenced coniferous plantation turn right and continue to another gateway leading out of Knole Park and into woodland. Climb hill and at a fourway intersection of footpaths continue straight ahead through woods to reach a lane. Turn left and after only a short distance fork right, following the lane signposted to Bitchet Common.*

5. *At an intersection continue straight across, following the lane past Falcon Cottage, Fawke House and Fawke Farm House. At the bottom of the hill, as the lane swings left, turn right into a dirt track and continue up the hill in the direction of a footpath sign through woodland. At a T-junction at the top of the hill turn right, following a bridleway flanked by a wooden fence, to reach One Tree Hill car park.*

ACCESS BY BUS
To Fawke Common from Sevenoaks.

interests of future generations. On a bright sunny day children waste no time adapting to their circumstances and games of frisbee or simply running amongst the colossal upturned stumps of fallen trees provide great enjoyment. It must be pointed out to them, however, that although the deer which wander the thousand acres of Knole Park are friendly and beautiful to see, they should not be approached. They do no harm and prefer to be left alone.

Knole House, reached by continuing straight instead of turning right into Chestnut Walk, takes its name from the knoll it stands on. The building, now the largest private house in England, was started in 1456 by Thomas Bouchier, Archbishop of Canterbury. Henry VIII took over ownership in 1532 before Elizabeth I gave it to Thomas Sackville, 1st Earl of Dorset. It is thanks to Lord Sackville that the public are invited to walk through these grounds, sharing not only relief from the pressures of the modern world, but also the regal atmosphere that is set deep in Britain's history and is preserved to this very day.

Refreshments A picnic is called for and could be enjoyed at various points along the route.

DALE FARM

Sevenoaks Weald

Outline   Sevenoaks Weald ~ Dale Farm ~ Wickhurst Manor ~ Bowzell Wood ~ Sevenoaks Weald.

Summary   Explorers both young and old can tackle this walk with a real sense of adventure. The rolling hills around Sevenoaks Weald, two miles south of Sevenoaks, are a picturesque combination of farm and woodland, offering a stimulating variety of interest. Children will love the quick-fire succession of stiles, narrow footbridges and further stiles, while parents can hopefully find time as they follow the rather lengthy route description, to enjoy the constantly changing views, the splendid well-established oaks and the many wildflowers, including purple clover, honeysuckle or perhaps the unforgettable sight of horses grazing in a field speckled yellow with buttercups.

Attractions   Picture a smiling couple driving a pony trap along Church Road or children playing cricket or running races on the green, perhaps with the welcome prospect of an ice-cream from the friendly corner shop. In the corner of a nearby field there may be a new-born calf, watched over by a couple of attentive cows. Look out for butterflies, squirrels, rabbits, horses and sheep. In June and July the haws and hazel nuts begin to swell on pretty hedgerows dotted with pink dog rose flowers. These are only some of the delightful aspects that give this quiet area its own very special charm.

   Many famous people have lived here. The beautiful 15th Century Wickhurst Manor was thought to have been a meeting place for conspirators in the days of its owner, Sir Harry Isley, who, together with his friend Sir Thomas Wyatt, eventually lost his head for his part in a rebellion against the proposed marriage of Queen Mary to Philip of Spain. The poet Edward Thomas once lived in Sevenoaks Weald, as well as his friend W. H. Davies, author of the Autobiography of a Supertramp.

   Situated at the southern end of the village, the 14th Century manor house of Long Barn, rumoured to be the birth place of William Caxton, was bought in 1915 by Harold Nicolson and Vita Sackville-West. Vita's ancestral home was Knole in Sevenoaks. In 1936 Charles and Ann Lindbergh bought the house. Charles had flown solo across the Atlantic nine years previously in a small plane called the Spirit of St. Louis. While living at Long Barn, Ann wrote a book called Listen, the Wind. After

continued on page 56

Route 12

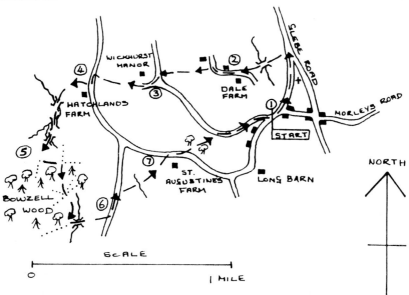

ROSEHIPS

54

Route 12

Sevenoaks Weald   4½ miles

START   *at the village green on the corner of Church Road and Windmill Road (O.S. Pathfinder 1208 G.R. 509527), approached by Morleys Road, off the A21. Limited parking near green.*

ROUTE

1. *Walk to end of Church Road, passing church on right. As Church Road leads into Glebe Road cross a stile on the left. Follow a footpath along left boundary of a field, continuing downhill and bearing left to cross over a stile. Proceed straight downhill along a path, cross a stream via a footbridge and then ascend slope on the other side.*

2. *Cross a stile and turn right into a farm lane. Follow lane between buildings of Dale Farm. Continue along lane as it swings right and just round the corner turn left and cross a stile into a field. Cross field diagonally towards the right and enter another field. Continue straight ahead, crossing another stile and pass through a narrow fringe of trees to enter another field. Continue downhill and then proceed up the other side of the hill, bearing slightly towards the right. Cross a stile and then after about twenty yards cross another stile into a field. Cross this field, bearing slightly left, before crossing another stile and then proceeding straight ahead through another field.*

3. *Cross a stile and turn left into a lane. After about ten yards, just before Cedar House, turn right into another farm lane. Proceed along length of this lane and, just to the left of a private driveway at the end, cross a stile into a field. Cross this field diagonally towards the left. At the far left corner of this field follow the path as it continues uphill between two other fields. Continue to top of hill and cross a stile, turning left into a tarmac lane.*

4. *As the lane bears left, just before driveway to Hatchlands Farm, turn right and cross a stile into a field. Cross field, bearing towards the left. Cross a stile and then a footbridge. Follow path as it swings left and then after about twenty yards cross another stile and another footbridge. Proceed along left boundary of a field and then cross a stile, closely followed by a narrow footbridge and then another stile. Continue all the way along the left boundary of another field to reach a stile in the far left corner beside a gate.*

5. *Cross this stile and turn left into a track. Continue along track through a gateway into woods. At a fork turn left and continue to an intersection of tracks. Turn right and then continue along path, going straight across*

another intersection. Follow track as it bears to the right, continuing through woods. At a T-junction of tracks turn left, crossing a stream before continuing uphill along a wide grassy walkway.

6. *At the top of the hill cross a stile and turn left into a lane. After about three hundred yards cross a stile on the right into a field. Cross the field diagonally towards the left. Cross another stile, step across a small stream and cross a second stile. Cross a field diagonally towards the right and then cross a further stile into yet another field. Continue across this field towards the barn of St. Augustine's Farm.*

7. *Just to the left of barn, pass through old kissing gate and turn right into lane. After about fifty yards cross a stile on the left and follow path downhill through a field and then up the other side, leading across a further stile into woodland. Follow path through woods before crossing another stile into a field. Walk diagonally towards the right across this field, bearing left at the corner of a private garden and continuing with the fence on the right. Cross another stile and turn right into a road, following it all the way back to the village green.*

ACCESS BY BUS
To Sevenoaks Weald from Sevenoaks and Bromley.

———

being used as a home for children evacuated from East London during the Second World War, the house was sold to a film producer called Paul Soskin. A later owner was another author, Arthur Koestler, who wrote The Sleepwalkers and The Lotus and The Robot.

Refreshments   At the Windmill pub or a picnic in Bowzell Wood.

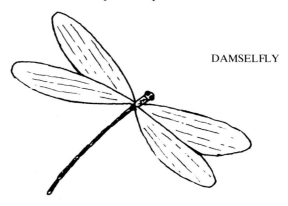

DAMSELFLY

Route 13

Ide Hill

Outline   Ide Hill ~ Octavia Memorial Seat ~ Chains Farm ~ Hanging Bank Lane ~ Ide Hill.

Summary   With the worthwhile exception of a short, but very steep climb towards the end of the route, this is a relaxing, easy walk, offering some of the most splendid views in Kent. From the sloping green above the village, perfect for a picnic or games with the children, the North Downs Way can be seen across the Holmesdale Valley towards the north, while from the National Trust viewpoint near the church on the other side of the Greensand Ridge the outlook stretches southwards across the Weald. The breathtaking panorama of Bough Beech Reservoir from the lofty car park may tempt the less energetic visitor to simply sit back and enjoy a quiet picnic without going any further, although as the paths and tracks lead beside fields and hedgerows or beneath the gnarled branches of mature oaks, sweet chestnuts, holly and ash, the extensive views continue to delight with constant surprises and interesting changes in perspective.

Attractions   Ide Hill is linked with Toy's Hill, Mariner's Hill and Crockham Hill, each hilltop bearing a memorial to Octavia Hill, co-founder of the National Trust. Sitting on the memorial seat, looking out across the silver waters of the Bough Beech Reservoir, while listening to birds singing in the trees, it becomes more apparent than ever that the lady of vision deserves a great deal of gratitude. Her thoughtfulness and concern for future generations has set a fine example.

There is no age barrier to the enjoyment of seeing the many farm animals along the way, with perhaps a trusting greeting from a pair of contented donkeys or a quizzical stare from a group of sheep. More careful observation will be required to spot a fox or a rabbit and the hedgerows and fields are alive with various kinds of birds, from pheasant and partridge to robin and chaffinch.

The evidence of storm damage is clear, especially on Toy's Hill, seen across the valley towards the right on the approach to the memorial seat. The open area is dotted with the deep pink flowers of the foxglove between June and September, a plant that quite literally does the heart good, having a medicinal property as a stimulant. Other flowers include the bright five-petalled yellow pimpernel, blossoming between May and August, the pale pink dog-rose, red-campion, sweet-smelling

continued on page 60

Route 13

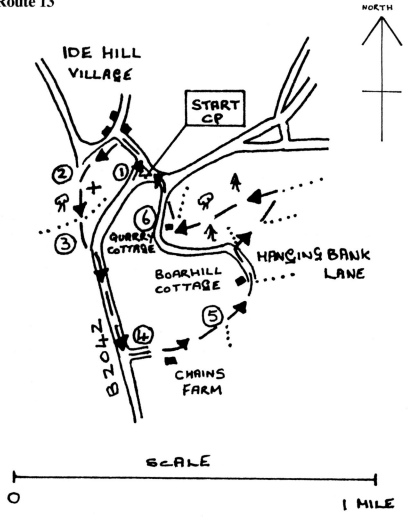

NORTH

IDE HILL VILLAGE

START CP

② ① ③ ⑥ ④ ⑤

QUARRY COTTAGE

BOARHILL COTTAGE

HANGING BANK LANE

CHAINS FARM

B2042

SCALE

0   1 MILE

Route 13
Ide Hill
2½ miles

START *from the car park on the Ide Hill Road (B2042) at the turning into Ide Hill Village (O.S. Pathfinder 1208 G.R. 517488), approached by the A25.*

ROUTE

1. *From car park turn right into lane, following direction of roadsign to Ide Hill and Sundridge. After about twenty yards turn left at an intersection and follow the lane uphill into Ide Hill Village. Just past the Cock Inn bear left and walk across the green towards the church.*

2. *Enter the National Trust via a signposted footpath to the right of the church and proceed along a tarmac track. After about a hundred yards take the signposted footpath to the right, as the track turns left into the Old Vicarage. Continue along a dirt track to reach a National Trust viewpoint. Keeping to the left, continue over the brow of the hill along a path which leads to the Octavia Hill Memorial Seat.*

3. *Follow footpath on the right of the memorial seat down a wooden stairway and then over a stile into a lane. Taking care of traffic, turn right and continue for ⅓ mile before turning left into a tarmac driveway, indicated both by a sign to Chains Farm and also by a small footpath sign.*

4. *Continue along driveway for several hundred yards before entering Chains Farm through a gateway. Keeping to the left, follow a short track through another gateway and then climb a stile into a field. Cross this field diagonally to the left, entering a smaller field through another gate. Keep to the right boundary and pass through another gate into another field. Skirt right border of this field, crossing a little stream, before reaching a stile at the far right corner.*

5. *Instead of crossing stile, turn left and follow edge of field uphill towards Boarhill Cottage. Cross a stile into a tarmac lane (Hanging Bank Lane) and continue uphill, taking a footpath to the right at a point where the lane swings sharply to the left. Continue along side of hill, taking the left turn at a fork in the path. Climb a steep slope and turn left into a track. Follow track until it swings sharply uphill to the right just before Quarry Cottage.*

6. *Continue to the cottage and then take the tarmac pathway which leads away towards the right. Proceed as pathway leads into lane. After a few yards turn left into Ide Hill Road and retrace steps to car park.*

honeysuckle and pink and purple rhododendrons, both in gardens and also in the wild.

Ide Hill Village is charming, peaceful and quaint. The Cock Inn dates back possibly to the 16th Century and the nearby school was designed by the Victorian architect George Edmund Street, who also designed the London Law Courts. Rosemary Cottage is early Georgian and the Old Vicarage, built with brick and ragstone, dates back to the 19th Century. Ide Cottage is believed to be a little older.

On the approach to Boarhill Cottage the path crosses over a small stream before unveiling a sloping field peppered with hillocks, the tops of which draw little children like magnets where they claim proudly and with challenge that they are the King of the Castle. An amused adult may consider that the silent victor of such a competition must surely be the nearby spire of Ide Hill Church, nearly 800 feet above sea level, making it possibly the highest in the county.

Along the path leading to the car park from Quarry Cottage the odd peep into several gardens, which in turn look out over the valley of the Weald, will provide a final touch to set the memory firmly in the mind, something to beckon the visitor back one day.

Refreshments   At the Cock Inn, The Crown, or a picnic either on the green or perhaps the National Trust viewpoint.

ACCESS BY BUS
To Ide Hill from Sevenoaks.

DRYHILL PICNIC PARK

Route 14

Dryhill

Outline Dryhill Picnic Park ~ Monks Well ~ Sundridge Church ~ Dryhill Picnic Park.

Summary Apart from several rather high stiles, this is a short, easy ramble through the countryside, keeping away from busy roads and villages, making it an ideal choice for those in search of peace and relaxation. With three farms along the route, Wellers Farm, Sundridge Place Farm and Warren Farm, the rustic atmosphere is complete and children will be delighted by the constant array of animals including horses, sheep, cattle and possibly even little lambs and calves, staring back at them with their large, innocent eyes. A good pair of binoculars may enhance some of the far-reaching views as well as possibly helping to pick out the occasional wilder animal such as a deer or perhaps one of the many birds like robins, pheasant, partridge or that most well-known of British land birds, the chaffinch. The month of May is notable for the unforgettable displays of white and later pink hawthorn blossom, draped profusely and yet delicately like lacework over rich green foliage.

Attractions Visitors may feel the odd twinge of envy mingled with a sense of wonder as they turn the corner of Dryhill Lane beside the beautiful garden of White Sheiling and the grounds beyond belonging to the Barn, the Dry Oast and Dryhill Farm. This beautiful area owes some of its charm to the wide variety of trees, another memorable sight being the tunnelled avenue of ash, hawthorn and coppiced hazel which leads down a gentle slope to the wooden-fenced paddocks of Warren Farm.

In addition to the interesting variety of cultivated plants to be seen during the short stroll through the nurseries near Smarts Garden Centre, there is an abundance of wildflowers on the route, including the pink flowering herb Robert, stitchwort, speedwell and the pretty purple common vetch.

Just before the ascent to Sundridge church, via an ancient flight of stone steps, the route passes through a field, the highest point of which is known as The Toll, from where monks used to keep watch in times of religious persecution. It is now a known vantage point, offering sweeping views over the Holmesdale Valley and also the gap where the Darent River flows between two sections of the North Downs Way. All that remains of a priory that used to stand near The Toll is a stone-enclosed cave, built around a spring five hundred years ago, called Monks Well, now a watering point for farm animals.

continued on page 64

61

Route 14

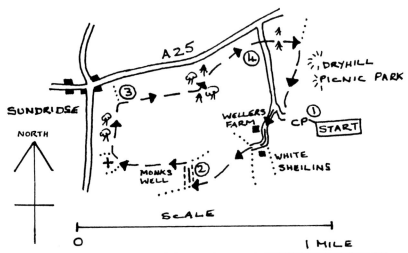

THE BARN, DRYHILL

Route 14

Dryhill

2½ miles

START   *at the Dryhill Picnic Park (O.S. Pathfinder 1208 G.R. 552497), approached by Dryhill Lane off the A25.*

ROUTE

1. *Leave the car park of the Dryhill Picnic Park and turn left into Dryhill Lane. Continue past Wellers Farm, following the lane as it bears right at the gateway of White Sheiling. Continue uphill, ignoring a stile to the right and proceeding straight ahead into a signposted public bridleway (also indicated by a blue arrow numbered 225) at a point where the lane swings away to the left. Follow bridleway, ignoring another stile on the left, before meeting a farm track.*

2. *Turn right into track and continue as it bears left. Just before it bends again, this time to the right, continue straight on, crossing a stile into a field. Continue straight across field, passing Monks Well and then ascending a flight of stone steps to enter churchyard through a kissing gate. Take the right-hand fork, bearing right again at a second fork in the path to leave the churchyard via a second kissing gate. Follow path along the left edge of a field.*

3. *At the far corner ignore a stile which leads straight on and turn right instead, continuing along the boundary of the field. Continue straight through three more fields, via two stiles, before crossing a third stile into a wooded footpath which swings sharply to the left. Continue downhill through a coppiced avenue before turning right into a track. At the end of the track cross a stile into a field.*

4. *Proceed through nurseries, cross a stile and then continue straight across Dryhill Lane into the car park of the Sigas Showroom. The footpath leaves the back of this yard via a stile behind a row of conifers. Cross a field and enter a second field by crossing a small footbridge. Turn right and continue along the edge of this field to the far corner. Cross a stile into a small band of woodland, before emerging into Dryhill Picnic Park.*

ACCESS BY BUS
To Dryhill Lane from Sevenoaks and Bromley.

The section of Dryhill Picnic Park just inside the entrance is surrounded by trees with a large open space, which is ideal for children's games of rounders, football or cricket. Barbecues are permitted in this area too, a tempting way to end what could be a perfect outing.

There are also two possible extensions to this walk. The first is through the churchyard into Sundridge to see the 15th Century Old Barn and the War Memorial, or perhaps to take refreshment at the White Horse pub. The second is by way of a footpath at the back of the Dryhill Picnic Park which leads into Chipstead with its picturesque lake, once a sand pit and now home of The Chipstead Sailing Club. There are also many listed buildings in Chipstead, although it must be said that the crossing over the A21 should be treated with the utmost care. The speed of passing cars requires a quick adjustment from the lulling relaxation of the countryside.

Refreshments The White Horse pub in Sundridge or a picnic or barbecue at the Dryhill Picnic Park.

CHURCHILL STATUE

Route 15   3 miles
Westerham

Outline Westerham ~ Park Lodge ~ Lakes Walk ~ Quebec House ~ Westerham.

Summary Westerham, a market town by royal decree since 1227, is centred around a small triangular green presided over by the statues of two heroes, General James Wolfe and Sir Winston Churchill. Visitors may wish to browse in one of the interesting antique shops or perhaps an exclusive boutique. They may want to linger in a charming tea shop, or a friendly pub. However, the objective of the outing shouldn't be allowed to slip comfortably away. The route through Squerryes Park is memorable. There are also two perfect picnic spots, one overlooking the young Darent, which rises in the grounds of the nearby Crockham House, and another above Tower Walk, overlooking the length of the valley. The wide fenced pathway on the western bank of the park is tailor-made for children to run up and down, a handy practice for the grassy slopes on the sides of Lakes Walk, while the playground in St. George's Field is an added bonus.

Attractions To the right of the pathway along the southern boundary of the town there are beautiful gardens, with white benches around a private lake, little wooden footbridges over streams, colourful flowerbeds and croquet hoops on a well-tended lawn. At the end of this path a crossing over a bridge presents the walker with a lovely pond, possibly with ducks bobbing on its surface. Higher up on the western side of Squerryes Park there is a splendid view back over Westerham and the hills that rise to the North Downs beyond.

    The route continues through a delightful wooded field of beech, oak, sweet chestnut, holly and birch before descending, with the spectacular view ahead of the Crockham Hill Woods, to a quiet corner where the River Darent runs gently between Tower Wood and the sloping meadows of the park. The hovering electric blue damselfly might be spotted here along with butterflies and playful swifts.

    The garden of Glebe House, to the right of the path on the return to Westerham, is a flame of colour in late May or early June, with purple and scarlet rhododendrons and yellow and orange azaleas. Along the route in early summer there also are sprays of white elder flowers and later in the year clusters of black elderberries.

    The town is perhaps best known for its war heroes, General James Wolfe and Sir Winston Churchill. General Wolfe was born at the

continued on page 68

Route 15

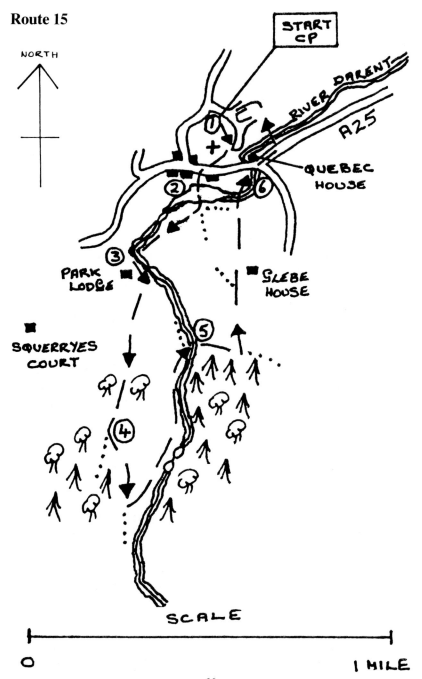

NORTH

START CP

RIVER DARENT

A25

QUEBEC HOUSE

② ⑥

③
PARK LODGE

GLEBE HOUSE

SQUERRYES COURT

⑤

④

SCALE

0   1 MILE

66

Route 15

Westerham   3 miles

START   *at car park in Westerham on the corner of Quebec Avenue and London Road (O.S. Pathfinder 1208 G.R. 541448), approached by A25.*

ROUTE

1. *Leave the car park in the direction of a sign to the town centre. Proceed along a footpath for several hundred yards and then turn right, continuing uphill through the churchyard. On leaving the churchyard bear left and cross the green, passing the statue of Sir Winston Churchill before crossing the A25. Climb a few steps leading to a tarmac footpath between Owl House and The Clothes Gallery.*

2. *Proceed along footpath to reach the River Darent (a small stream at this point). Cross over once via a stone step and then a second time about thirty yards further on via a wooden bridge. Continue straight and then cross over a stile, taking the footpath to the right. Continue with gardens on the right and sloping grassland to the left. At the end of this path cross the Darent again via a stile followed by a footbridge, then turn left into a track.*

3. *Continue along track and then cross a stile to the right just beyond Park Lodge. Follow footpath up a hill and cross another stile. Continue along a track bordered with fences on both sides before crossing over a further stile. Proceed through a field, cross yet another stile and then walk through a wooded field before crossing a further stile.*

4. *Turn left into a farm track and continue over the brow of a hill and down the other side. At the bottom cross a stile to the left into a field, in the direction of a signpost to Lakes Walk. Follow path as it leads into another track and then bears left, running alongside the River Darent. Continue until track reaches a gate and then cross a stile. Turn right and walk beside the fence towards the stream in the direction of a signpost to Tower Walk.*

5. *After about fifteen yards cross a stile and then a bridge. Continue along a pathway, keeping to the right edge of a field. At the far right corner of this field turn left instead of continuing straight ahead over a stile. Climb a steep hill and then continue straight on, keeping to the right edge of the field, passing Glebe House on the right and crossing a stile halfway down the slope. At the far right corner leave the field via a footpath and after about thirty yards cross the Darent via a footbridge. Twenty yards*

further on cross a stile and walk through a small band of woodland leading into Mill Street.

6. *At the end of Mill Street cross A25 and turn right, continuing past Quebec House and Cope's Oyster House before turning left into a footpath. Follow path as it swings left and then after about fifty yards turn right. Cross the Darent via a footbridge into St. George's Field and walk through children's playground. Leave the recreation ground via a gate opposite the bowling green and cross through a car park into a lane. At the end of this lane turn right into Quebec Avenue and retrace steps to car park.*

ACCESS BY BUS
To Westerham from Sevenoaks and Bromley.

———————

Vicarage in 1727 and grew up at Spiers, later renamed Quebec House in honour of his famous victory in Canada in 1757, when he sailed up the St. Lawrence to attack Quebec and scaled the heights of Abraham. The story of the battle is illustrated by an exhibition in the old stable block at the back of Quebec House. Four rooms within the house are open to the public with displays of some of his personal effects from snuff box to dressing gown. The 15th Century house, built of brick and Kentish ragstone was left by its Canadian owner, Joseph Bowles Learmont of Montreal, to the National Trust on his death in 1913. As a child General Wolfe often visited Squerryes Court and a cenotaph in the grounds now marks the spot where at the age of fourteen he received his first military commission, delivered by courier from Whitehall.

Between 1929, when the Conservative government was defeated, and 1939 when he was recalled as First Lord of the Admiralty, Sir Winston Churchill lived with his family at Chartwell, two miles south of Westerham, where he is known to have enjoyed writing, painting and renovating the estate. It was with his own hands that he built the wall around the kitchen garden and also part of a cottage. He also designed a section of waterfalls and rock pools. The house, now owned by the National Trust, contains a large display of memorabilia, as well as many of his paintings in the studio where he created them.

Refreshments At one of many pubs or tea rooms in Westerham or a picnic on the route.

Route 16   4 miles

Crockham Hill

Outline Crockham Hill ~ Buttle Steps ~ Froghole Lane ~ Crockhamhill Common ~ Mariners Hill ~ Crockham Hill.

Summary A rabbit hopping across a meadow through a flock of sheep too busy grazing the lush green grass to even notice, an orange-winged butterfly flitting across the path, a squirrel elegantly springing to a temporary observation point on top of a wooden fence, the drone of bees nosing in and out of purple and creamy-white foxgloves, the rich aroma of fern leaves mingling with the heady sweetness of honeysuckle, wisteria and roses, just a handful of reasons which could easily make an early summer walk through this area seem like a stroll through paradise. Children will enjoy running through wide open spaces, clambering over little hills and darting in and out of some of the many tracks in Crockhamhill Common. Particularly exciting are the huge bushes of rhododendrons, making a tunnel at one point over the path. Parents can look on with their own sense of wonder as the vast splashes of purple flowers make the very air glow with a delicate lilac hue.

Attractions In the churchyard of the 19th Century Holy Trinity Church is the grave of Octavia Hill, co-founder of the National Trust. Although she was offered a tomb in Westminster Abbey, it was her wish to be buried in the area she loved and where she spent the last remaining years of her life.

The tiny village of Crockham Hill, situated on the slopes of the Greensand Ridge, about two miles south of Westerham, has its own school and post office, the latter doubling up as a surprisingly well-stocked general store. The Royal Oak pub, which apparently used to display its own well in the public bar, is part of a row of terraced houses, which form the original village at a point where there was a toll gate across the road until 1866.

The walk begins by crossing two meadows divided by a footbridge beneath a beautiful oak. The appearance of the meadows confirm reports that because the porous greensand rock absorbs rainwater, the water reservoirs below, which are held by beds of clay, sometimes get too heavy, causing the ground to buckle. During dry weather the water level drops and with it the floating meadows above! In 1596, over a period of eleven days and with a great deal of noise, it is reported that the area changed dramatically in shape.

continued on page 72

69

Route 16

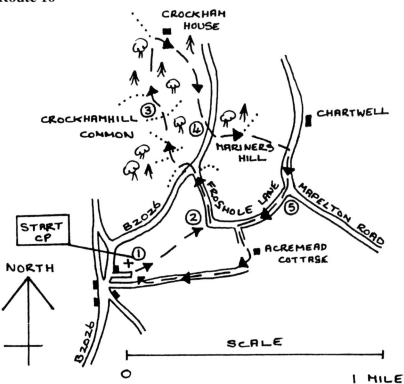

FROGHOLE FARM

Route 16

Crockham Hill

4 Miles

START   *at the Holy Trinity Church car park (O.S. Pathfinder 1208 G.R. 507444), at the end of lane leading to church off B2026, approached by A25.*

ROUTE

1. *Cross the stile at the bottom corner of the car park and walk straight along a footpath through a meadow with the churchyard on the left. Cross another stile and then a footbridge over a stream. Continue along footpath which skirts left boundary of another meadow. At far left corner cross another stile and follow footpath which leads up a winding staircase through a series of gardens to Froghole Lane.*

2. *Turn left and continue uphill to end of Froghole Lane. Climb steps to the right for a diversion to the top of Mariners Hill or cross over B2026 and take footpath directly opposite. Follow path as it bears left, passing a garden on the right before reaching a fork. Turn right and continue uphill into the woods, passing a path to the left and a few yards later one to the right, before reaching another fork. Take right fork, following blue arrow indicating Greensand Way. On reaching an intersection of paths, continue straight across and then follow path as it bears to the left.*

3. *As path widens, continue for two hundred yards before turning right into a footpath beside a fence. Cross a stile and continue downhill along path, crossing a second stile before reaching the bottom of the slope. Turn right just before a third stile, following path in direction of footpath sign to Froghole Lane. Proceed all the way to the entrance to April Cottage and turn left, following driveway to B2026.*

4. *Cross lane and follow footpath opposite in the direction indicated by a blue GW arrow, number 367. Climb steep hill, passing a wooden post bearing another blue arrow. On reaching a fork keep to the right, passing Windmill Bank Cottage and then continue straight downhill to reach Mapleton Road. A diversion to the left leads to Chartwell. Otherwise turn right and continue down lane, passing Old Well Cottage on the left. Just beyond this point enter through a swing gate on the right, indicated by a public footpath sign in front of another cottage. This leads into a private road to Mariners.*

5. *Continue to end of private road, going through gateway into Froghole Lane. Continue uphill before turning left into a narrow lane indicated by a sign to The Coach House. Proceed to end of lane and continue*

along a footpath straight ahead. Follow path downhill through woodland to reach Acremead Cottage on the left. Turn right in front of the neighbouring driveways to Chandlers and The Coach House. Proceed along lane past several cottages and gardens, crossing the third stile on the right and then following a path through a small band of woodland to reach the car park.

ACCESS BY BUS
To Crockham Hill from Westerham (very infrequently).

———

Towards the right from this point there is a far-reaching view across the Weald, while ahead and slightly to the left are the double oasts of Froghole Farm. Youngsters won't be able to resist counting the steep winding steps, known as Buttle Steps, which climb through lovely tumbling gardens to Froghole Lane. Older members of the family may appreciate the profusion of wildflowers beside the steps.

At the end of Froghole Lane there are steps leading to the National Trust viewpoint of Mariners Hill. Turn right at the top of the steps to reach a memorial seat looking westwards towards Surrey. For picnic-lovers this spot is perfection itself. Just behind the bench the path continues over the top of the hill, offering panoramic views both to the south and east. Crossing the B2026, the walk passes through Crockhamhill Common, with its oaks, birch, ash and conifers. The descending slope on the far side offers a view northwards into Squerryes Park and the path leading back to the B2026 allows the odd peep into the grounds of Crockham House where the River Darent has its source.

Another optional diversion on this strenuous, but highly rewarding walk, is to the former home of Sir Winston Churchill, which is about a quarter of a mile to the left on reaching Mapleton Road. Chartwell, originally called Atwell after the owner of a farmhouse on the site in 1352, became the property of John Colquhoun in 1848. He transformed it into a mansion, before Churchill bought it in 1921, subsequently adding to the splendour of the gardens with waterfalls and a dam dividing two lakes.

Refreshments   At the Royal Oak pub or a picnic on the route.

Appendices

ROUTES IN ORDER OF DIFFICULTY

Starting with the easiest:

Route 5 — *Eynsford - 3½ miles*
Route 11 — *One Tree Hill - 3 miles*
Route 1 — *Keston - 2½ miles*
Route 14 — *Dryhill - 2½ miles*
Route 13 — *Ide Hill - 2½ miles*
Route 4 — *Chelsfield - 4½ miles*
Route 3 — *High Elms - 4½ miles*
Route 12 — *Sevenoaks Weald - 4½ miles*
Route 15 — *Westerham - 3 miles*
Route 8 — *Kemsing - 4½ miles*
Route 10 — *Shipbourne - 4½ miles*
Route 9 — *Oldbury Hill - 4 miles*
Route 7 — *Otford - 5 miles*
Route 6 — *Shoreham - 4 miles*
Route 2 — *Cudham & Downe - 4½ miles*
Route 16 — *Crockham Hill - 4 miles*

PUBLIC TRANSPORT IN NORTH-WEST KENT

The area covered by this book is fairly well serviced by public transport although careful study of timetables is essential since some services tend to be infrequent.
For details of operators and timetables contact the following:

Auto Reps .... Tel. 0474 534078
British Rail .... Tel. 071 928 5100
Green Line .... Tel. 081 668 7261
Kent County Council .... Tel. 0622 671411
(Highways & Transportation)
Kentish Bus Company .... Tel. 0732 462316
Maidstone & District .... Tel. 0634 847334
Metrobus Ltd .... Tel. 0689 861432
Selkent .... Tel. 081 318 7421
Sevenoaks Bus Station .... Tel. 0732 453596

TOURIST INFORMATION CENTRES IN NORTH-WEST KENT

Maidstone, The Gatehouse, Mill Street. Tel.0622 602169.
Rochester, High Street. Tel. 0634 43666.
Sevenoaks, Buckhurst Lane. Tel. 0732 450305.
Tunbridge Wells, Town Hall. Tel. 0892 26121.

WET WEATHER ALTERNATIVES IN NORTH-WEST KENT Completely or partly under cover.

It is advisable to check times of opening before a visit is made.

MUSEUMS AND CRAFT WORKSHOPS

Bromley Arts Council, Sundridge Avenue, Bromley. Tel. 081 464 5816; concerts, displays and art exhibitions. Open: details of events obtainable from the council.
Bromley Museum, The Priory, Church Hill, Orpington. Tel. 0689 831551; local history including display of tools from Mesolithic (Middle Stone Age) found in Priory Gardens. Open: everyday except Thursdays and Sundays.

Haxted Mill, near Edenbridge. Tel. 0732 862914; working mill and museum. Open: April to May, Bank Holidays and weekends, June to September afternoons.

Whitbread Hop Farm, Beltring, Paddock Wood. Tel. 0622 872068; working hop farm with museum, craft centre, children's play area and pets corner. Open: Easter to October. Refreshments.

Shoreham Countryside Centre, Shoreham Railway Station; local history and geography, displays and information on local flora and fauna. Open: weekends and Bank Holidays. Refreshments.

Ightham Vineyards, Ivy Hatch, near Sevenoaks. Tel. 0732 810348; phone for details of tours and winetasting.

Penshurst Vineyards, Penshurst. Tel. 0892 870255; tours, meals and winetasting. Open: all year.

Sevenoaks Museum, Buckhurst Lane, Sevenoaks. Tel. 0732 452384; collection of objects and photographs of local interest. Open: everyday except Tuesdays and Sundays.

Craft Centre of Silk, Bourne Road, Crayford. Tel. 0322 59401; a journey through time along both The Old and The New Silk Routes with replica dockside, block-makers' shed, hand-screen printing workshop, Victorian street and shop. Open: daily except Sundays and Bank Holidays. Refreshments.

Dartford Museum, Market Street. Tel. 0322 343555; local history, displays including the priceless Darenth Bowl, unique early Christian glassware dating from A.D.450. Open: weekday afternoons (except Wednesdays) and all day Saturday.

The Old Laundry, High Street, Westerham. Tel. 0959 63237; needlework, wool and craft centre. Open: daily.

Elan Arts Centre, Ide Hill. Tel. 0732 75344; local craftware and also a range of national and international giftware. Open: Wednesday to Sunday. Refreshments.

CASTLES, HOUSES AND CHURCHES

Ightham Mote, near Sevenoaks. Tel. 0732 810378; medieval moated manor house. Open: April to October except Tuesdays and Saturdays.

Knole, Sevenoaks. Tel. 0732 450608; one of England's largest private houses containing one of the world's most important collections of 17th Century furniture. Open: April to October.

Quebec House, Westerham. Tel. 0959 62206; General Wolfe's childhood home and Tudor stable block containing an exhibition about the Battle of Quebec. Open: April to October except Thursdays and Saturdays.

Old Soar, near Borough Green; late 13th Century solar block. Open: April to September.

St. John's Jerusalem Garden, Sutton-at-Hone; garden and remains of a commandery of the Knight's Hospitallers. Open: April to October, Wednesday afternoons.

Stoneacre, Otham Village. Tel. 0622 86186; a 15th Century half-timbered manor house. Open: April to October, Wednesday and Saturday afternoons.

Emmetts Garden, near Ide Hill. Tel. 0732 75367; five-acre hillside garden with tearoom. Open: April to October, Wednesday to Sunday and Bank Holiday Monday.

Chartwell, near Westerham. Tel. 0732 866368; home of Sir Winston Churchill from 1924-1965. Open: April to October.

More information on the above can be obtained from the National Trust.

Hever Castle, near Edenbridge. Tel. 0732 865224; 13th Century castle and ornamental gardens, once the home of Anne Boleyn. Open: end of March to November afternoons only.

Leeds Castle, near Maidstone. Tel. 0622 765400; medieval castle and gardens with aviary. Open: April to October daily and November to March weekends only.

Down House, Downe. Tel. 0689 59119; Charles Darwin's home for forty years, now a memorial museum. Open: March to January afternoons except Mondays and Fridays.

Squerryes Court, Westerham. Tel. 0959 62345; William and Mary manor house built in 1681. Also, 18th Century garden and displays of paintings, tapestries, furniture and porcelain. Open: April to September Wednesdays, Saturdays, Sundays and Bank Holidays.

Lullingstone Castle, Eynsford. Tel. 0322 862114; home of the Hart Dyke family. Frequent visitors included Henry VIII and Queen Anne. Display of family portraits. Open: April to September weekends and bank holidays.

Chiddingstone Castle, near Edenbridge. Tel. 0892 870347; former seat of the Streatfields, converted to a castle in about 1805. Special attractions include: The Royal Stuart and Jacobite Collections, Japanese Art, Armour and Swords, Egyptian Antiquities and Buddhist Art. Open: end of March to September.

Penshurst Place, Penshurst. Tel. 0892 870307; medieval hall built in 1340 with 15th Century extensions retaining their Gothic character. Former residence of kings and dukes surrounded by Tudor-inspired gardens. Also, Venture Playground and Toy Museum. Open: April to October, daily except Mondays.

Hall Place, Bexley. Tel. 0322 526574; part-Tudor, part-Jacobean country house. Stone from monasteries closed by Henry VIII was used to build the northern part of the house, while the southern part boasts one of the best moulded plaster ceilings of its period in Kent. Extensive garden and greenhouses. Open: telephone for details.

St. Paul and St. Peter church, Shoreham, with rood-screen bearing pomegranate emblem of Catherine of Aragon.

The Church of St. Martin of Tours, Chelsfield, the tower houses the oldest surviving peal of bells in Kent.

St. Botolph's church, Lullingstone, resting place of many of the Peche and Hart Dyke families.

Keston Church, Keston, part-Norman flint and stone church with a weeping chancel, built in 13th Century.

The Church of St. Peter and St. Paul, Seal, containing an interesting collection of memorial brasses reflecting lives of people in the area since 1395.

St. Mary the Virgin church, Kemsing, with the oldest brass of its kind in Kent as well as several small articles of plate.

The Church of St. Botolph, Chevening, dating from the 13th Century, with a perpendicular tower added 200 years later.

Church of St. Giles, Farnborough, flint and brick church which was rebuilt in 1639 after a storm. In the churchyard is the Boswell grave, a memorial to the Queen of the Gypsies.

Church of St. Bartholomew, Otford, extensively restored in 1863, Saxon in origin with 12th Century tower and later additions including 17th Century painted glass.

St. Mary the Virgin church, Downe, 13th to 15th Century flint church restored in 1872, with a sundial and plaque commemorating the life of Charles Darwin.

Church of St. Peter and St. Paul, Cudham, twice-restored 12th Century church with steeple containing four bells, two dating from 1661.

St. Mary the Virgin church, Ide Hill, built in 1865 with intricately-designed ceiling with corbels representing leaves of hops, chestnut and mulberry.

St. Giles church, Shipbourne, built in 1880, with Italian mosaic floor.

St. Mary's church, Sundridge, Early English building with tower and shingled spire.

St. Mary the Virgin church, Westerham, 16th Century, containing early royal arms of King Edward VI.

Holy Trinity Church, Crockham Hill, with a memorial effigy in the chancel of Octavia Hill, co-founder of the National Trust.

St. George's church, Sevenoaks Weald, built in 1820, with a chancel, designed by T. G. Jackson, added in 1872.

SPORTING FACILITIES under cover.
Beckenham Leisure Centre. Tel. 081 650 0233.
Walnuts Leisure Centre. Tel. 0689 870533.
Splash World Swimming Pool. Tel. 081 303 5781.
Profiles Spots & Leisure Club. Tel. 0689 826077.
Profiles Dry Ski Centre, (outdoors). Tel. 0689 878239.
Fanta Seas Water Park. Tel. Dartford 88811.
Bromley Sports Hall. Tel. 081 313 4300.
White Oaks Sports Centre, Tel. 0322 62188.

TRAINS, CAVES AND WILDLIFE ATTRACTIONS

North Downs Steam Railway, Dartford. Tel. 0322 228260; large collection of locomotives and rolling stock. Video show and souvenir shop. Open: March to November weekends. Refreshments.

Chislehurst Caves. Tel. 081 467 3264; guided tours through caverns and passages hewn out of the living chalk over a period of 8000 years. Reputedly used by Romans, Druids and smugglers. Open: Easter to September daily and September to Easter at weekends (also daily during school holidays).

Sevenoaks Wildfowl Reserve. Tel. 0732 456407; nature trail, hides, information centre and museum. Open: Wednesdays, Saturdays and Sundays.

Hollanden Farm Park, Hildenborough. Tel. 0732 832276; collection of rare farm animals, display of antique farming equipment, Iron Age settlement and adventure playground. Open: Easter to October. Refreshments.

Badsell Park Farm, Matfield. Tel. 0892 832549; pet area and animal farm. Also pick your own fruit, nature trail and bird and insect displays. Open: May to November. Refreshments. Picnic site.

Stone Lodge Farm Park, Dartford. Tel. 0322 343456; traditional working farm, producing dairy goods and wool by turn-of-the-century means. Also on summer Sundays experts demonstrate rural crafts. Open: all year. Refreshments. Picnic site.

BIBLIOGRAPHY

Frank W. Jessup, A History of Kent, 1958.
Frederick G. Wood, Let's Explore The River Darent, 1983.
Bromley Borough Council, Environmental and recreational leaflets, 1989/1990.
Shoreham Women's Institute, Shoreham Kent, A Village Booklet, 1988.
The Otford Society, Otford Mount and Greenhill, 1989.
William Webb, Kent's Historic Buildings, 1977.
Pat Davis, Leisure Guides Kent, 1989.
Madeleine Eattell, The People of The Parish of Seal 1820-1880, 1985.
Margaret Stevens, Past Generations of Seal and Kemsing, 1985.
Michael McNay, Red Guide Kent, 1989.
Muriel V. Searle, Hayes, West Wickham and Keston, 1988.
Kev Reynolds, A Visitor's Guide to Kent, 1985.
Alan Bignell, The Kent Village Book, 1986.
John Newman, West Kent and the Weald, 1969.
Sean Jennett, The Pilgrims' Way, 1971.
Reginald Turner, A Vision of England - Kent, 1950.
Pennethorne Hughes, A Shell Guide - Kent, 1969.
Arthur Mee, The King's England - Kent, 1969.
Sir Edward Harrison, The Story of Oldbury Hill, 1953.

A FRIENDLY WELCOME IN DOWNE (Route 2)

FAMILY WALKS SERIES

Family Walks in the Lake District. Barry McKay. ISBN 0 907758 40 1.

Family Walks in West Yorkshire. Howard Beck. ISBN 0 907758 43 6.

Family Walks in Three Peaks and Malham. Howard Beck. ISBN 0 907758 42 8.

Family Walks in South Yorkshire. Norman Taylor. ISBN 0 907758 25 8.

Family Walks in Cheshire. Chris Buckland. ISBN 0 907758 29 0.

Family Walks in the Staffordshire Peak and Potters. Les Lumsdon. ISBN 0 907758 34 7.

Family Walks in the White Peak. Norman Taylor. ISBN 0 907758 09 6.

Family Walks in the Dark Peak. Norman Taylor. ISBN 0 907758 16 9.

Family Walks in Snowdonia. Laurence Main. ISBN 0 907758 32 0.

Family Walks in Mid Wales. Laurence Main. ISBN 0 907758 27 4.

Family Walks in South Shropshire. Marian Newton. ISBN 0 907758 30 4.

Family Walks in the Teme Valley. Camilla Harrison. ISBN 0 907758 45 2.

Family Walks in Hereford and Worcester. Gordon Ottewell. ISBN 0 907758 20 7.

Family Walks in the Wye Valley. Heather and Jon Hurley. ISBN 0 907758 26 6.

Family Walks in the Cotswolds. Gordon Ottewell. ISBN 0 907758 15 0.

Family Walks in South Gloucestershire. Gordon Ottewell. ISBN 0 907758 33 9.

Family Walks in Oxfordshire. Laurence Main. ISBN 0 907758 38 X.

Family Walks around Bristol, Bath and the Mendips. Nigel Vile. ISBN 0 907758 19 3.

Family Walks in Wiltshire. Nigel Vile. ISBN 0 907758 21 5.

Family Walks in Berkshire and North Hampshire. Kathy Sharp. ISBN 0 907758 37 1.

Family Walks on Exmoor and the Quantocks John Caswell. ISBN 0 907758 46 0.

Family Walks in Mendip, Avalon and Sedgemoor. Nigel Vile. ISBN 0 907758 41 X.

Family Walks in North West Kent. Clive Cutter. ISBN 0 907758 36 3.

Ready Spring 1992

Family Walks in the Weald of Kent and Sussex
Family Walks in North Yorkshire
Family Walks around Luton and Dunstable
Family Walks in Northumbria
Family Walks in Nottinghamshire
Family Walks on the Isle of Wight
Family Walks in Clwyd
Family Walks in Dorset
Family Walks in Rossendale, Pendle and Bowland

Other titles under consideration

The Publishers, D. J. Mitchell and E. G. Power welcome suggestions for further titles in this Series; and will be pleased to consider other manuscripts of Derbyshire and regional interest from new or established authors.
